Comprehensive Sericulture: From Cocoon to Commercial Silk

Aarthi Nekkanti
&
**J. Komal

Preface

Sericulture, the craft of producing silk, has been a vital part of human history for centuries. From the humble silkworm cocoon to the luxurious fabric we know as silk, this process has evolved into a sophisticated industry that blends tradition with modern technology.

Comprehensive Sericulture: From Cocoon to Commercial Silk is designed to offer a clear and concise overview of the entire silk production process. This book covers everything from the biology of silkworms to the latest techniques in silk reeling and processing. It also addresses the economic and environmental aspects of the silk industry, making it a valuable resource for students, professionals, and anyone interested in this fascinating field.

We hope this book provides you with the knowledge and inspiration to explore the world of sericulture and its many possibilities.

Aarthi Nekkanti
&
J. Komal

Acknowledgments

The journey of writing *Comprehensive Sericulture: From Cocoon to Commercial Silk* has been an enriching experience, made possible by the support, guidance, and encouragement of many individuals. I would like to express my sincere gratitude to everyone who contributed to this work. First and foremost, I am deeply thankful to my mentors and colleagues, whose expertise and insights have significantly shaped the content of this book. Your willingness to share your knowledge and experiences has been invaluable, and we are honoured to have learned from such esteemed professionals.

Special thanks go to my family and friends, whose unwavering support and understanding have been crucial in the completion of this book.

Finally, I would like to acknowledge the publishers for their professionalism and dedication in bringing this book to life. Your efforts in refining the manuscript and ensuring its publication have been greatly appreciated.

To everyone who has played a part in the creation of this book, thank you. It is our hope that *Comprehensive Sericulture: From Cocoon to Commercial Silk* will serve as a valuable resource and contribute meaningfully to the ongoing study and practice of sericulture.

SERICULTURE

- ❖ **Introduction to Sericulture**
  - ➢ The word '**Sericulture**' is derived from the **Greek 'Sericos'** meaning '**silk**' and the English '**culture**' meaning '**rearing**'
  - ➢ It involves the cultivation of **mulberry** to produce leaf, rearing of silkworm to convert leaf to cocoon, reeling of the cocoon to obtain silk yarn and weaving to convert yarn to **fabrics**
  - ➢ Silk is a **natural** fibre where two independent **fibroins** called brins are completely covered with **sericin**
  - ➢ The **7th of August** is commemorated as **National Handloom Day** in India
  - ➢ Also known as "**Queen of textiles**" and "**Biosteel**"
  - ➢ The **Mysore** and **North Bengaluru** is known as '**Silk City**' of India
  - ➢ India's **biggest** cocoon market is situated at – **Ramanagara** cocoon market
  - ➢ **Silk Samagra** - Inegrated Scheme for Development of Silk Industry for 3 years from **2017 to 2020.** It is an Integrated Scheme for Development of Silk Industry has been able to sustain and strengthen the Sericulture activities in the country.
  - ➢ In collaboration with the **TATA Steel Foundation**, the district administration in **Jajpur (Odisha)** is reviving **Asia's largest sericulture** farm at **Sukinda.**

- ❖ **History of Sericulture**
  - ➢ Silk was discovered in **China** by the Empress, **Si- Ling** and later spread to other parts of the **world.**
  - ➢ The first authentic reference to silk is found in the Chronicles of the **Chou- King of China (2,200 BC)**
  - ➢ **Story behind silk discovery:** The king is reported to have pointed out to the Empress Si-Ling the worms destroying the mulberry trees in his garden. As she tried to gather the cocoons, she accidentally dropped one of them into a bowl of hot tea. While trying to recover the cocoon from the hot liquid with a spoon, she discovered that a very fine and very long lustrous thread unwound itself from the cocoon. She discovered silk and the process of obtaining it from the cocoons.

- From **China**, the secret of silk making spread first to **Korea** through Chinese immigrants in **1,200 BC.** From there it spread to **Japan**, when Semiramus, the Japanese General conquered Korea
- From **China**, the secret of sericulture spread to **Tibet** when a Chinese Princess, who married the King of Khoten, carried mulberry and silkworm seeds in her head apparel
- From **Tibet**, it spread to **India** in l40 BC
- Each sericultural state in India has a traditional reputation for a particular kind of silk **goods** from ancient times. Eg. **Banaras silk**, **Kashmir silk**, **Bengal silk**, **Mysore silk** and **Kanchipuram silk**

❖ **Silk Road**

- The Silk Road was a prestigious network of trade routes linking the civilization of the **East** represented by **China** with the civilization of the **West** represented by **Rome**
- The **6,400 km** long Silk Road (actually a caravan tract) started in Sian followed the Great Wall of China, Afghanistan, Syria, Egypt, Mediterranean ports to Europe
- In **2014**, after years of preparation among countries, the property of the Silk Roads: the Routes Network of Chang'an-Tianshan Corridor was inscribed on the **World Heritage List**
- To strengthen international cultural exchanges and promote the spread of Silk Road culture, 2021 Silk Road Week held its opening ceremony at **China** National Silk Museum in Hangzhou, Zhejiang province, on **June 18**

❖ **Organizations in sericulture industry**

- International Sericulture Commission (ISC) was established in **Lyon**, **France** in the year 1948 and shifted **Bangalore 2013**
- International Congress on Sericulture and Silk Industry is going to held from 7-11th Sep, **2022** with New Concepts in Sericulture *"SERITECH"* at Cluj-Napoca, **Romania** (University of Agricultural Science and Veterinary Medicine)
- Central silk Board (**CSB**) established in **1949** is one of the earliest statutory bodies of the government of India, with its headquarter located in **Bangalore**, under the **Ministry of**

Textiles which is the **apex body** responsible for promotion and over all development of sericulture and silk industry in India

➢ **Silk Mark** organization of India (**SMOI**) is a registered, society, sponsored by the CSB, which gives **'Silk mark label'** to the silk goods. These are affixed only on **pure silk** products by the authorised users of Silk Mark

➢ **The institutes under CSB are**

Central silk board	Bangalore
Central sericultural research & training institute	Mysore
Central silk technological research institute	Bangalore
Central sericulture research station	Behrampur, Orissa
Central Tasar research station	Ranchi, Bihar
Central Muga & Eri research institute,	Lahdoigarh, Jorhat, Assam

❖ **GOODS AND SERVICES TAX (GST) –For Silk Sector**

ITEMS	DESCRIPTION	GST
Silkworm cocoons	Suitable for Reeling	0%
Raw silk	Not Thrown (Un twisted/Not thrown)	
Silk Waste	Reeling/Spinning /Weaving waste including waste cocoons	
Silk yarn	Spun silk, twisted (Mulberry / Tasar / Muga) silk, Noil, silk embroidery Yarn	5%
Silk Fabrics	Sarees, handloom/power loom woven fabrics, other silk fabrics Ready Made Garments etc.	5% & 12%

	Garment value is < Rs.1000/- = 5% Garment Value is > Rs.1000/- = 12%	
Silk Machinery	All types of Reeling, twisting, spinning Weaving, Testing Machinery	**18%**
Silk Handloom Machinery	All types of Handlooms (Weaving machinery)	**0%**
Silk Testing Services	Technical Testing & analysis services	**18%**
Silk Expos	Events, Exhibitions, Conventions and trade shows organisation and assistance services	**18%**

❖ **Types of Silkworms**

Mulberry Silkworm (Bombycidae)	1. ***Bombyx mori*** is **domesticated** silkworm, feeds on **mulberry** leaves belonging to family Moraceae 2. These are classified and identified as uni-voltine, bi-voltine, and multi-voltine races and they are of pure and hybrid strains 3. The worms produce long, continuous silk filament which is white or light yellow in colour. The silk has good commercial value

Tasar Silkworm (Saturniidae)	1. Tasar silkworms are of **three** types.
	  I. ***Antheraea mylitta*** - Feeds on *Terminalia tomentosa* and reared in India
	  II. ***Antheraea proylae*** - Feeds on Oak leaves and reared in India

	III. *Antheraea yamamai* - Feeds on Arjun, Sal, Oak, and Plum, reared in Japan 2. These are **Uni** or **Bi-voltine** types 3. Cocoons are big in size and weigh about 7-14 grams with a **peduncle** and reeled to get **1000-1200** meters of fiber 4. The silk is highly valued for its **quality**
Eri Silkworm **(Saturniidae)**	1. The scientific name of Eri Silkworm is *Philosamia ricini* and it is a **domesticated** silkworm, reared on **Castor** and **Tapioca** leaves. 2. It produces a white or **brick-red Silk** 3. The Eri silk filament is neither continuous nor uniform in thickness, thus cocoons **cannot be reeled**. 4. Therefore, the moth emerged from cocoons are used to extract silk by process of spinning but not reeling. So, the pupae are not killed, so called as **'ahimsa silk'**.
Muga Silkworm **(Saturniidae)**	*1.* The scientific name of Muga Silkworm is *Antheraea assamensis* 2. feeds on **Som** and **Soalu** leaves to produce **Golden – yellow silk** thread which is very strong and attractive 3. It is the unique monopoly of India found in Brahmaputra Valley and adjoining hills in **Assam** 4. The rearing is done **outdoors**
Anaphe Silkworm **(Notodontidae)**	1. **Anaphe** is a polyphagous **Insect** and feed on 22 varieties of food plants 2. It is a **uni-voltine** silkworm which is **green** in colour 3. The silkworm of genus **Anaphe** is found in southern and central Africa which produces the silk. Approximately **12-100** larvae form collective cocoons (**spin in communes**) enclosed by thin layer of silk.

	4. This soft and fairly lustrous silk is more elastic and stronger than mulberry silk. The silk is used in **velvet** and **plush** (crafting, needlework) making.
Fagara Silkworm (Saturniidae)	*1.* **Fagara** silk is obtained from the giant silk moth *Attacus atlas* *2.* It belongs to the family **Saturniidae** **3.** It is the largest of the living insects reaching up to eleven inches in wing-span **4.** **Less important** since the silk is not commercially exploitable.
Coan Silkworm	1. Coan silk fibre is secreted by the larvae of *Pachypasa otus* **2.** This is a polyphagous insect feeding on pine, ash, cypress, juniper and oak **3.** In ancient times, this silk was used to make crimson dyed apparel worn by the **dignitaries of Rome**
Mussel Silkworm	1. Mussel silk, a non-insect type of silk is obtained from a particular bivalve mollusc like *Pinna squamosa* **2.** The fibre is called **byssus** thread, which is brown in colour, strong in quality and keeps the animal to anchor itself to a rock or any surface of the habitat **3.** The **byssus** is combed and then spun into a silk popularly known as **fish-wool**
Spider Silkworm	1. The **spider silk** is a **non-insect variety**. **2.** The **soft** and **fine spider** silk is noted for its strength and elasticity. The commercial production is obtained from **Madagascan** species. **3.** Because of **high cost** of production this silk is not used in Textile Industry, but it is used as gill nets, dip nets, kite nets and various lures for the fishing activities and also for weaving bags, caps and head dresses.

❖ **Types of Silkworms**

	Mulberry	Eri	Tasar	Muga
Domestication	Domesticated	Semidomesticated	wild	Semidomesticated
Voltinity	Bivoltine/Multivoltine	Multivoltine	Multivoltine	Bivoltine
Colour of the silk	White	Brick red	Brown	Golden yellow
Main hosts	Mulberry	Castor	Terminalia	Som & Soalu

❖ **Chromosome Number (2n) of different types of Silkworms**

Types of Silkworms	Chromosome Number (2n)
Bombyx mori	56
Antheraea mylitta	62
Antheraea prolei	60
Bombyx mandarina	54
Muga silkorm	30
Eri Silkworm	28
Wild Eri Silkworm	26

❖ **Host plants of different Silkworms**

Types of Silkworms	Host plants
Mulberry Silkworm	Mulberry (Monophagous)

Tasar silkworm	*Terminalia tomentosa* (Asan)
	Terminalia arjuna (Arjun)
	Shorea robusta Roxb. (Sal)
Muga silkworm	Som (*Persea bombycina*)
	Soalu (*Litsaea polyantha*,Juss)
	Mezankari (*Litsaea citrate*)

MORICULTURE

- ➤ Scientific cultivation of mulberry is called as "**Moriculture**"
- ➤ Mulberry – origin – **northern hemisphere** (Himalayan foot hills)
- ➤ Mulberry was cultivated in 2800 BC by Chin–nong taught cultivation of mulberry in China
- ➤ There are about 68 sps. of genus Morus
- ➤ Family- **Moraceae**
- ➤

Morus alba	**Grown throughout India**
Morus indica	
Morus latifolia	
Morus nigra	
Morus laevigata	**Grown in Himalayan region**
Morus serrata	

- ➤ Most of the Indian varieties belong to *Morus indica*
- ➤ *M. nigra* has highest chromosome no – **308 chromosomes**
- ➤ *M. indica* is of superior quality used for research purpose but low yield

❖ **Morphology of Mulberry**

- ➤ Mulberry is a fast growing – **Deciduous – Woody – Perennial tree – Deep rooted taproot system**
- ➤ Leaves are alternate (both lobed & serrated leaves)
- ➤ Each node bears buds one vegetative bud and the other reproductive bud
- ➤ Inflorescence – **Catkin**/Spike (Monoecious/ Dioecious)
- ➤ Fruit of mulberry- **Sorenson**.
- ➤ Pollination by – **Wind**

❖ **Climatic conditions required for mulberry**

Atmospheric Temperature	24°C to 37°C
Rainfall	600 mm to 2500 mm
Atmospheric Humidity	65 to 80 percent
Sunshine	5 to 10 hrs a day.
Elevation	Japan- 22m to 1735m MSL. U.S.S.R. – 400m to 2000m MSL. India- 300m to 700m MSL
Soil type	Loamy
Soil pH	6.5 to 7.0.

❖ **Propagation**:

    1. Seeds

    2. Cuttings of 22-23 cms length with 3-4 buds (Pencil thickness)

❖ **Mulberry varieties**

I. Local cultivar	
Mysore Local	1. The **Mysore Local** variety is commonly called the local or **naatikaddi** was once extensively cultivated in traditional sericultural tracts of Karnataka. 2. It is comparatively low yielding variety, but known for its adaptability to low agronomic inputs and poor management practices, both under rainfed and irrigated conditions. 3. Leaves are smooth, **heterophyllous** with both lobed and unlobed leaves occurring in the same plant, alternately or spirally arranged, ovate- broadly ovate, palmately veined and membrane like 4. Leaf yield is about **8000 kg and 25000 kg/ha/yr** under rainfed and irrigated conditions respectively.
II. Improved cultivars	

M5 or K-2. Kanva-2 (K-2) or Mysore-5 (M-5)	1. It is an **open pollinated hybrid (OPH)** selection from the seedling population of **Mysore local** variety. 2. The selection was done in the **Kanva** Silk Farm near **Channapatna** during late 1950s. It grows vigorously and responds well to agronomical practices. 3. Leaf yield is about **10000-12000 kg/ha/yr** with **10 tons** of **FYM** and **100:50:50k** NPK/ha/yr
MR2	1. **Mildew Resistant variety-2** was developed by Tamilnadu Sericulture Department at their experimental Station, Coonoor during 1970s. 2. This is resistant to powdery mildew caused by *Phyllactinia corylea* and is very popular in plains of Tamilnadu and better suited for both plains and high-altitude areas where high temperature prevails. 3. It yields **25,000 to 30,000kg** leaf/ha/yr. under irrigated conditions of **Tamilnadu**
III. High yielding varieties	
S30	1. Open type bushes, branches are simple, vertical, rough and greenish grey with short internodes. 2. Leaf yield is about **35,000 kg/ha/yr** under **irrigated conditions** with recommended package of practices.
S36	1. Bushes are of open type, branches are simple, vertical, rough and greenish grey with short internodes. 2. Leaf yield is about **42,000 kg/ha/yr** under irrigated conditions with recommended package of practices. 3. Owing to its better leaf succulency and higher nutritive value, it is specially recommended for **chawki rearing.**
Vishwa (DD)	1. Vishwa variety is the selection from the collections of **Dehradun** area of Uttar Pradesh where mulberry grows naturally from open pollinated hybrid seedlings.

	2. This variety has good sprouting and rooting ability with fast growth, suitable for **5-6 crops per year.** 3. Leaf yield is about **45,000 kg/ha/yr**
V1 (Victory-1)	1. V1 variety bushes are of open type, branches are simple, vertical, rough and with short internodes. 2. Leaf yield is about **60,000 kg/ha/yr** under **irrigated conditions** with recommended package of practices. 3. Performs better in wider spacing. 4. The recommended spacing is **paired row system**
G-2	1. The variety was evolved in 2003 for irrigated conditions for raising mulberry gardens exclusively for **young age silkworm rearing.** 2. The variety yields **38-40 MT leaf /ha/year.**
G–4	1. G4 is an elite mulberry variety evolved in 2003 for irrigated conditions specifically and for **late age silkworm rearing.** 2. The variety yields **55-60 MT leaf/ha/year.**
IV. Varieties for specific conditions	
A. Alkaline condition	
AR-11	1. The variety was evolved in 1999 for rainfed and semi-arid conditions or areas with limited irrigation. 2. This variety yields **8-10 MT leaf/ha/year**
AR-12	1. The variety was evolved in 2000 for alkaline soils with **pH > 8.5.** 2. This variety yields **25 MT leaf/ha/year**
B. Resource constraint	
RC-1	1. This variety evolved in 2002 is suitable for sub optimal conditions (**at least 50 % reduction** in water and manures). 2. It yields **24-26 MT leaf/ha/year.** This variety is suitable for late age silkworm rearing
RC-2	1. This variety evolved in 2002 is suitable for sub optimal conditions (**at least 50 % reduction** in water and manures).

	2. It yields **24-26 MT/ha/year**. This variety is suitable for **late age silkworms.**
C. Shade tolerant variety	
Sahana (K2 x Kosen)	1. This grows well **under shade** in a coconut garden in peninsular states of India.
	2. This variety yields **25 MT leaf/ha/year**

❖ **Different Mulberry varieties for different geographical conditions**

Irrigated Conditions	K2 (M5), S-54, S-36, V-1, G-2, G–4
Rainfed conditions	S-13, S-34, RFS-135, RFS-175
Temperate	Goshoerami, China white
Sub-temperate	Chakmajra, S-146
hilly regions of north and north-eastern India	S-1, S-7999, S-1635, S-146, Tr-10 and BC-259

❖ **Mulberry planting system**

➢ The inter plant and inter row distance recommended for tropical countries is **3ft x 3ft** in rainfed and **2 x 2** for irrigated crop and temperate regions like Kashmir it is **4ft x4 ft.**

➢ **Planting systems**

Pit system	1. Plantation method was recommended by **CSRTI**, Mysore in 1980s.
	2. Pits of 35 x 35 x 35 cm size are made at a spacing of 90 x 90 cm.

	3. **10 tons** of organic manure/ha such as cattle dung compost is recommended to apply under rain fed conditions.
	4. Three healthy cuttings should be planted in each pit in a triangular form with a distance of 15cm.
	5. Care should be taken to expose only one bud.
	6. In case of saplings, one sapling is enough per pit.
	7. The roots propagate fast and plants establish fast.
	8. A hectare of mulberry garden contains **12,345 plants**
Row system	1. Under irrigated conditions, plantation is taken up in pit system as well as row system. While planting under irrigated conditions the recommended variety of mulberry suitable to the area is taken up.
	2. In the row system of plantation, the rows one made 60 cm apart. cuttings or saplings are planted in the rows at a distance of **22 cms.**
	3. In the pit system the rows are made 60cm apart and cutting or saplings are also planted at a distance of **60cm**.
	4. Ridges and furrows should be made at a distance of **60cm**.
	5. The furrows should be **15cm**. deep. Cuttings should be planted along the margin of ridges.
Paired row system	1. The paired row plantation for mulberry was developed and introduced at **CSRTI, Mysore** in 1995.
	2. It facilitates movement of power tillers and tractors for intercultural and other operations in a mulberry garden. This system of plantation reduces dependency on man and animal power for intercultural operations.
	3. **(5'+3') x 2'** is the most common paired row plantation system adopted by a large number of farmers. Here, the distance between two rows of pair is 90 cm (3'). The space between two pairs is 150 cm (5').

	4. The plant-to-plant space in a row is 60 cm (2'). The total number of plants per hectare is **13, 437.** 5. The mechanized cultivation improves the quality of leaves and curtails expenditure on intercultural operations by at least by half.
3M planting	1. The 3M plantation is modification of **90x90 cm** (3'x3') plantation where the movement of tractor operated machinery is not feasible. 2. In 3M Plantation, the mulberry plants are placed in blocks where each block contains 9 plants. 3. In each block the plants are spaced **at 90 cm** from each other as shown in the schematic diagram. 4. The blocks are separated from each other **by 120 cm.**
Kolar system	1. Under irrigation, the row planting known as **"kolar system"** is followed. In this system rows and furrows are made at a distance of **30 to 45 cm.** 2. On either side of ridges mulberry is planted at a distance of 10 to 15cm between the plants along the row. 3. This is followed in the **kolar district** of **Karnataka** and so is called the **kolar system.**
Strip system	1. This is very close system of mulberry cultivation is practiced in **West Bengal** where mulberry is grown in strips. 2. Each strip has either two rows (**Dothaki**) or three rows (**Thethaki**). 3. Each strip is separated from adjacent strip by wide distance so that harvesting and inter cultivation and other operations can be done using small tractors or other machines.

	4. Within the strip, plants are planted at a distance of **15 cm** between the rows and between the two plants within the row.
Angular system	1. This is a new system of cultivation evolved by **RSRS, Conoor** for the slopes of the **Nilagiris**. 2. The distance between the plants is similar to the pit system that is **90cm** but the plants in adjacent rows are planted in such a way that they form a **triangular** arrangement. 3. This system is claimed to allow more plants per unit area better soil and moisture conservation, efficient cultural operations, increased leaf production, better supervision and efficient and economic water management.

> Planting season: july - august (onset of monsoon)
> Planting method: Planting can be done in a pit, row or paired row system.
> Cuttings should be from a healthy main shoot with **three sound buds**.
> They should be planted in a **slanting position** with one bud above the ground level. Saplings raised in the nurseries can also be used for planting in the main field.

❖ **Spacing:**

a) Pit system (under rain fed condition)- 3' x 3' (90 X 90 cm)

b) Row system (irrigated condition)

3' x 3' (Heavy soils, deep black cotton soils and heavy rainfall area)

2' x 2' (Plain land)

4'x 2' (Sloppy lands in hilly areas)

c) Closer system or Kolar system (irrigated condition) - 2' x 1', 1' x 1', 1.5' x 1'

d) Paired row system or strip system (irrigated) – 6 x (3 x 2), 5 x (3 x 2), 4 x (2 x 1)

❖ **Manuring**

- ➤ **10 to 12 tons** of FYM or compost per hectare for **rainfed**
- ➤ **20 to 25 tons** of FYM or compost per hectare for **irrigated garden** should be given at the time of annual pruning or as a basal dose.
- ➤ Fertilizers: Recommended fertilizers Kg Per hectare per year. a) **Rain fed** mulberry garden – N: P2O5:K2O (**100:50:50**) (N:P: K in the ratio **of 2:1:1)**
- ➤ **50:50:50** kg of NPK has to be given as a **basal dose** and remaining **50 kg** of N is given as top dressing after the first leaf harvest.
- ➤ **Irrigated mulberry** garden (NPK in the ratio of **2.5:1:1** applied in 5-6 split doses corresponding to leaf harvests)

> **Shoot harvest**: N:P: K (300:120:120)
>
> **Leaf harvest**: N:P: K (280:120:120)

- ❖ **Foliar sprays for mulberry**

The growth regulator-based sprays	1. **Vipul** consisting of **triacantnol** a 30- carbon alcohol has been used as a plant growth regulator in mulberry fields and is reported to result and is reported to result in an increase in growth and yield of leaves. 2. **Seriboost** is a commercial formulation containing essential **Micronutrients** and growth promoting substances like **n-triacontanol** required for Mulberry. 3. Spraying of **"Morizyme-B"** a plant growth regulator can also be done on mulberry leaf by dissolving 1 ml of it in 1 litre of water (0.1 %) during sunny days twice for better quality of leaf production particularly during winter under irrigated as well as in rainfed conditions.
Micro nutrient-based sprays	1. **Poshan** is a multi-nutrient formulation

	2. Foliar spray of **Poshan** results in 20% increase in leaf yield, besides improving leaf quality

* ❖ **Bio-fertilizers**
  - ➢ The use of bio-fertilizer like "**Nitrofert**" that contain bacteria called *Azotobacter chroococcum* at the rate of **20 kg /ha/year** in irrigated mulberry cultivation can save the application of chemical nitrogen fertilizer by **50 %** besides keeping the soil free from chemical pollution.
  - ➢ However, in case of rainfed and hilly regions the recommended dose of "**Nitrofert**" is **10 kg/ ha/ yr.**
  - ➢ the use of **VA-mycorrhizal (VAM)** bio-fertilizer called "**Phosphofert**" is also highly useful in mulberry cultivation. It helps the plants to absorb phosphorus rapidly from the soil through the symbiotic association of mulberry roots with certain fungi.
  - ➢ By use of this, it is possible to reduce the application of phosphorus by **60- 80%.**
  - ➢ The dose of **phosphofert** recommended for irrigated mulberry is **75 kg / ha/ 4 years.**
  - ➢ Under **rainfed** and **hilly condition**, the dose is recommended to be **38 kg/ ha/ 4 years** and applied at the root zone of the individual plant
  - ➢ Irrigation should be given at least once in **8 days** for **sandy loam** soils, **10 days** for **red loamy** soils**, 12** for **black clay soils.**
  - ➢ **Mulching**: Pruned mulberry branches can be spread in between mulberry rows as good surface mulch. Green manure crops like **cowpea, Horsegram, Sunhemp** or **Dhaincha** in between mulberry rows should be grown, which also serves as mulch.

* ❖ **Pruning**
  - ➢ **Bottom pruning or low-cut pruning:** Rain fed mulberry shoots should be pruned during July month at a height of 10-15 cm above the ground level to produce profuse branches and maximum bush development. This is referred as bottom pruning or annual pruning
  - ➢ **Middle pruning:** During winter, the mulberry shoots are cut at a height of 2½ to 3' or about 1 meter (middle pruning).

- ➢ **Top pruning or high cut pruning:** In irrigated mulberry garden, under closer spacing the shoots should be pruned to the soft portion at 4 to 6" height above the ground after the first leaf harvest and thereon.
- ➢ **Kolar system:** Branches are cut to the ground level, where in the pruning and harvesting are done together.

❖ **Harvesting and Yield**

- ➢ Different methods of harvesting include:
    - a) **Leaf picking**
    - b) **Branch cutting**
    - c) **Whole-shoot harvest**
- ➢ The first leaf harvesting (leaf picking) in rain fed garden is done after **10 weeks** of pruning followed by 7-8 weeks intervals.
- ➢ **Hand picking of leaves** – chawki rearing
- ➢ **Branch cutting** – 3rd instar larvae
- ➢ **Top shoot harvesting** – 4 th and 5th instars
- ➢ About **5-6 harvests** can be done in a year.
- ➢ An average of **6000 to 8000 kg** of leaves can be obtained per annum per hectare.
- ➢ Irrigated mulberry is generally harvested by shoot harvest at 8-10 weeks intervals.
- ➢ Thus, about five crops in a year can be raised and **30000 kg** of leaf per hectare per year can be obtained.
    - ➢ Selection of leaves: Suitable leaves are harvested depending on the larval instar:
        - **I instar:** top 3rd, 4th, 5th leaves
        - **II instar:** top 4th, 5th, 6th leaves
        - **III instar:** top 5th, 6th, 7th leaves
        - **IV & V instar:** mature leaves

❖ **TYPES OF MULBERRY PESTS**

Name of the pest	Symptoms of damage

Sucking pests	
Mealy bug: *Maconellicoccus hirsutus* **(pseudococcidae) Hemiptera**	1. The leaves are wrinkled, thickened, dark green and become yellowish prematurely. 2. Heavily attacked plants have shortened/condensed internodes leading to **'bunchy top or rosette'** appearance. The symptom is popularly known as **'tukra'.** 3. A heavy, black sooty mould also develops on attacked plants due to heavy deposition of honeydew produced by mealy bug.
Thrips: *Pseudodendrothrips mori,* **(Thripiidae) Thysanoptera**	1. Nymphs and adults of thrips make deep tunnels in the epidermal leaf tissues Affected leaves show **streaks** in the early stages and patches in the advanced stage
Jassids: *Empoasca flavescens* **(Cicadellidae): Hemiptera**	1. The pest serves as a **vector** for a toxic virus. 2. Yellowing / drying of leaves all along the leaf margin (**'hopper burn'**) due to injection of toxic virus. 3. The leaf becomes cup shaped and withers-off prematurely
White Fly: *Aleurodicus disperses,* **Aleyrodidae, Hemiptera**	1. Majority of the feeding damage is done by the **first three nymphal stages.** 2. The pest infests the lower surface of leaves resulting in **chlorosis** (paleness), yellowing and upward curling of the leaves. 3. Premature leaf falls and retardation in plant growth. 4. The attacked leaf becomes **unfit** for silkworm rearing
Leaf Eaters	
Leaf roller, *Diaphania pulverulentalis,* **Pyralidae Lepidoptera**	1. The target area of attack is the **apical portion** of the mulberry shoot.

	2. The young caterpillar **binds together the tender leaves** by silky secretion, settles inside and devours the soft green tissues of the leaf.
	3. Grown up caterpillars feed on tender leaves and their faecal matter can be seen on the leaves below the affected portions.
	4. Causes **10-12%** leaf yield loss
Bihar Hairy Caterpillar, _Spilosoma obliqua,_ Erebidae, Lepidoptera	1. The young caterpillars feed on chlorophyll layer of the leaf exposing the veins, which give **dried/mesh** appearance to the leaves. 2. The grown-up larvae feed on the entire leaf rendering the branches **without leaves.**
Cutworm, _Spodoptera litura,_ Noctuidae Lepidoptera	The larvae attack the shoots of young plants and cut them
Root / Shoot Feeders	
Stem borer, _Apriona spp._	1. Presence of holes on the stem / branches which leads to the **galleries/tunnels** made by the **boring** larva. **2. Withering** followed by drying up of attacked branches.
Termites, _Odontotermes spp._ Termitidae, Isoptera	1. They construct **earthen sheath** on the stem and feed on the bark. **2.** They also make **subterranean galleries** and feed on the roots. Small to bigger earthen mounds above and below the soil.
May–June beetle, _Holotrichia serrata,_ Melolonthinae, Coleoptra	1. Branches without leaves at different places. **2.** Drying up of the plants due to damage to **roots** and **rootlets** **3.** Reduction in leaf yield.

❖ **MULBERRY DISEASES**

Diseases of mulberry	Symptoms of damage
FOLIAR DISEASES	
Leaf Spot Disease Pathogen: *Cercospora moricola*	1. Brownish irregular spots appear on the leaf surface. 2. Spots enlarge and join together leaving characteristic **'shot hole'.** 3. Leaves become yellow and wither off as disease becomes severe
Powdery Mildew Disease Pathogen: *Phyllactinia corylea*	1. White **powdery patches** appear on the lower surface of the leaves. 2. The corresponding upper surface shows yellowish lesions. 3. When the disease is severe, the white powdery patches turn to brownish-black; the leaves become yellow, coarse and lose their nutritive value.
Leaf Rust Disease Pathogen: *Cerotelium fici*	1. Initially, small circular brown eruptions (outgrowths) appear on the leaves and later leaves become yellow and wither-off
Fungal leaf blight Pathogen: *Alternaria alternata* and *Fusarium pallidoroseum*	1. The disease starts as browning/ blackening of leaves from tips or margins of leaf. When severe, the entire leaf surface becomes brown and falls
Bacterial leaf blight Pathogen: *Pseudomonas syringae, Xanthmonas compestris*	1. Numerous blackish-brown irregular water-soaked patches appear on the leaves resulting in rotting of leave
SOIL-BORNE DISEASES OF MULBERRY	

Nursery Diseases	
Stem-canker **Pathogen:** *Botryodiplodia theobromae*	1. The disease appears as greenish-black eruptions on cuttings. The bark decays and dies.
Cutting **rot** **Pathogen:** *Fusarium solani*	1. The disease appears as decaying of bark and then rotting of the whole cutting resulting in death of the sprouted cutting
Collar **rot** **Pathogen,** *Phoma sorghina* **or** *P. mororum*	1. The disease appears as brown or black discolouration of bark and rotting of cuttings near the soil
Die-back **Pathogen:** *Botryodiplodia theobromae*	1. The saplings start wilting from the tip downwards resulting in death of the saplings
Root **Knot** **Disease,** *Meloidogyne incognita*	1. The severely affected mulberry plants show stunted growth with yellowing of foliage at leaf margin. 2. Formation of **knots/galls** on the roots is the underground symptom. 3. Young, spherical and yellowish-white galls appear on roots. Old galls are big and pale brown. 4. They are often mistaken with **root nodules.** 5. **Root galls** are bulging of roots at different places and root nodules appear on the root surfaces.
Root Rot Disease *Fusarium solani*	1. Initially, the disease appears as sudden withering of plants. 2. Leaves falloff from bottom 3. The roots turn black due to the fungus and decay 4. The plants loose the hold in the soil and can be easily uprooted. 5. On severity, the entire root system gets decayed and the plants die. 6. Affected plants after pruning, either fail to sprout or the plant, if sprouted, bears small 7. and pale-yellow leaves with rough surface

❖ **Integrated management of mulberry diseases and pests**

- **For nursery diseases** dipping of cuttings in Dithane M-45 (0.1%) solution and application of bioformulation called as **Nursery-Guard** prepared by using *Trichoderma pseudokoningii* (a product of CSRTI, Mysore)
- **For root knot nematode** soil application of **Bionema** (produced by using *Verticillium chlamydosporia*) mixed with Farm Yard Manure (FYM) and Neem oil cake in the ratio of 1:200:24 in 30-32 litres of water @ 200g / plant three times a year is an integrated approach for these diseases.
- **Navinya** - a **plant-based** formulation for management of **root rot** disease of mulberry (CSRTI, Mysore)
- **Nemahari** - a **plant-based** formulation for management of **root knot disease** of mulberry
- For control of pink mealybug, *Maconellicoccus hirsutus*, Release lady bird beetles, *Scymnus coccivora* **@500 beetles** or *Cryptolaemus montrouzieri* @ **250 beetles/ac/year** in two splits at an interval of 6 months
- For classical Biological Control of papaya mealybug, *Paracoccus marginatus* inoculative release of exotic nymphal parasitoid, *Acerophagus papayae* @ 1 vial (about 100 adults)/acre in pest infested gardens and other alternate host plants such as Papaya, Parthenium, Jatropha, Hibiscus, etc.
- For control of Bihar hairy caterpillar, *Spilarctia obliqua*, release *Trichogramma chilonis,* an egg parasitoid **@ 4 trichocards/acre/crop**

❖ **Life cycles of different species of silkworms (Bivoltine and Multivoltine)**

- The silkworm passes through four important stages (**Egg, Larva, Pupa and Adult**) during its life cycle.
- The life cycle is completed in **six to eight weeks** depending on climatic and racial characters.
- In nature **uni-voltine**, **bivoltine**, **multi-voltine races** are confined to different bio-geographical parts. Among them **multivoltines** of **tropical areas** have the **shortest** life cycle.

- The **uni-voltine races** produce only **one generation** in summer and the second-generation Eggs undergoes **hibernation** till next spring.
- In Bi-voltine races the third-generation eggs undergoes **hibernation** thus producing thus only **two crops** in a year.
- In the case of **multi-voltine** are **non-hibernating** thus yields as many as **seven to eight generations** in a year in tropical sericulture areas. The **multi-voltine** races have the **shortest** life cycle because of warmer ecological conditions and the rearing activity continues throughout the year.

Stage	Univoltine	Bivoltine	Multivoltine
Embryonic period	11-14 days	11-14 days	9-12 days
Larva	24-28 days	24-26 days	20-24 days
Pupa	12-15 days	12-15 days	10-12 days
Adult	6-10 days	6-10 days	3-6 days

❖ **Egg Stage**

- The duration of egg stage in the life cycle depends on diapausing or non-diapausing eggs. The diapausing eggs remain dormant under natural conditions for months together till spring of next year.
- This diapause can be broken artificially by **acid treatment (HCl),** after which eggs are **incubated** at a constant temperature for **11-14 days** for hatching.
- The temperature **(24-25 degree C)** provided during **incubation** favours the embryonic development of the egg to larva. While the **non-diapausing** eggs normally hatch in **9-12 days** period.

Diapausing Egg	1. Also called **"kuradone eggs"** 2. Eggs remain in dormant stage 3. It is Produced by the 2nd generations of **univoltine** silkworms and 3rd generations of **Bivoltine** Silkworms

	4. Eggs are dark brown before entering to diapause
Non- Diapausing Egg	1. Also called **"Nomodane eggs"**
	2. Eggs are **not dormant**
	3. It is Produced by **multivoltine** silkworms
	4. No color change but turns bluish before hatching

❖ **Larval Stage**

➢ This stage is important to the rearer since the complete crop yield depends on the various physiological process of the larva.

➢ The larval life may last from **20-24** days in **multi-voltine** species in **tropical areas** or **24-28 days** in **uni and bivoltine** races in **temperate areas**.

➢ The larval life of the worm is divided into five respective stages known as **5 Instars** and **4 moults**, so as to accommodate the growth that takes place in each instar, the feeding period.

➢ Thus, the larva casts off its skin and develops a new one to enter into succeeding instar.

➢ During this long period of feeding the larvae grows to **8,000 to10,000 times** compared to newly hatched worm.

➢ The first three instars are referred as **"young age"** or **"Chawki worms"** and fourth and fifth instars as **"late age"** worms.

❖ **Cocoon - Pupa**

➢ The mature and ripen worms spin the cocoon immediately after mounting and completes the spinning process in **48-72 hrs.**

➢ In another day or two the worm transforms into pupa within the cocoon.

➢ Pupa is an **inactive stage** where the larval structures degenerate and adult structures differentiate.

➢ The pupal period may last for **8-10 hrs.** The differentiated adult emerges slitting through the pupal skin, and piercing the final fibrous cocoon shell by releasing a **mild protease**.

❖ **Adult Moth**

- Adult moth exhibits sexual dimorphism like larvae and pupa. These moths are ready to copulate immediately after emergence.
- Adults' life span is **very short** and last for **3-10 days** depending on the season and races. Adults do not feed and **incapable of flight.**
- The females are with **broad abdomen** and males have **narrow abdomen**. The female lays about **400 eggs** after copulation with **male.**

Morphology of Bombyx mori

- ❖ **Morphology of life stages**
- ➢ **Egg Stage:**

1. The silkworm eggs are tiny and weigh around **2000 (1 egg weight is 0.5 mg)** eggs to a gram.
2. It measures **1-1.3 mm in length and 0.9 – 1.2 mm in width.** The size, weight, shape, colour of the egg, number of eggs per laying vary among the different races and according to the season.
3. The eggs of **European races** are comparatively **larger** and **heavier**. An average **Indian cross breed multi-voltine** races lays about **400 eggs** per laying.
4. The Eggs are ovoid, ellipsoid or oval and flat on one side this is called **egg dimple**. Races producing **white cocoons** lay **pale yellow eggs** while **yellow cocoons** lay **deep yellow eggs.** The Japanese races lay **slightly darker eggs** than **Chinese races.**
5. In **diapausing eggs**, the egg colour changes after 24 hrs of egg laying and becomes dark brown or purple with deepening of the colour of the seasonal pigment, but in non –hibernating eggs the colour does not change.
6. The protective covering of the egg is called **Chorion**, which has an opening called **micropyle** at the anterior end. There is a thin membrane called **Vitelline membrane** inside the chorion.
7. The vitelline membrane covers the **protoplasm** and the **yolk**. The yolk is not present throughout the egg but present just below the **vitelline membrane.**
8. A thin layer of cytoplasm does not contain the yolk and this portion is called the **Periplasm** which is particularly thick around the micropyle. This area is called an anterior polarplasm and contains the **egg nucleus.**

➢ Larval Stage

1. The newly hatched larva is black or dark brown in colour measuring **about 3 mm** in length.
2. It is commonly called as **ANT or KENGO**.
3. The head is large and the body is densely covered with bristles.
4. As the larva grows by passing moults to enter into later instars the body becomes smooth and light in colour due to rapid stretching of cuticular skin.
5. The body has 3 divisions i.e., **head, thorax, abdomen.**
6. The thin elastic chitinous cuticle permits rapid growth of the larvae during any instar.
7. **Sexual Markings:**

Male	1. A single median opening at the junction of the 8th and 9th segments called opening of **Herold's gland**. 2. It becomes the seminal duct and Ejaculatory duct of the adult
Female	1. A pair of sex marks on the ventral side of the **8th and 9th abdominal** segments called **Ishiwata's** Fore glands and **Ishiwata's** Hind glands respectively 2. Fore glands later modify to form the '**Bursa copulatrix**' and '**Receptaculum seminis**' 3. Hind glands become part of the **posterior region** of the oviduct and the accessory glands.

➢ Pupa or chrysalis

1. The pupal stage is generally called the **resting**, inactive stage of the silkworm when it is **incapable** of feeding and appears motionless. The pupal stage is a transitional phase during which definite changes take place.
2. During this period of biological activity the larval body and its internal organs undergo a complete change (Metamorphosis) and assume the new form of the adult moth.

3. The mature silkworm larva passes through a short transitory stage from pre-pupa to a pupa stage. During the pre - pupa stage the dissolution of the larval organs takes place and this is followed by the formation of the adult organs during the pupa stage.

4. Soon after pupation the pupa is white in colour and soft, but gradually turns **brown to dark brown** and the pupa skin harden

5. The prominent morphological parts visible are a pair of **large compound eyes, a pair of large antennae, fore and hind wings and the legs.**

6. Ten of the abdominal segments are seen on the ventral side when nine are seen from dorsal side. **Seven pairs of spiracles** are found in first seven segments and last pair is non-functional.

7. **Sexual Markings**

Male	1. **Pupa** is thinly built with **narrower abdomen** 2. There is a small **round spot** on the **9th segment**
Female	1. Pupa is larger with a **broader abdomen** 2. There is a **vertical line** in the centre of the **8th abdominal segment** on the ventral side

➤ **Adult Stage**

1. The adult moth emerging from the pupa is incapable to fly.

2. It does not feed during its **short adult life.**

3. The body of the moth is composed of three distinct segments i.e., **Head, Thorax and Abdomen.**

4. The adult body surface is covered with **scales.**

5. **Sexual Markings**

Character	Female	Male
Colour	Paler	Darker
Activity	Less active	More active
Antennae	Small	large
Body size	Large	small

Abdomen	Large and flat with 7 segments	Long, narrow with 8 segments
External genitalia	The caudal end has a median knob – like projection with secondary hairs. This knob is protruded and retracted to expel the pheromone	The caudal end has a pair of hooks known as **harpes** helping in copulation

❖ **Silk worm anatomy and physiology of digestive system**

➢ In the silkworm larva, the digestive system is more or less a straight tube from the mouth to the anus divided into three main parts: the **foregut** or **stomodeum**, mid gut or **mesenteron** and hind-gut or **proctodeum**.

➢ The oral aperture opens into the mouth cavity which is followed by a narrow **pharynx** and **oesophagus**. The **oesophagus** is narrow at the anterior end and gradually widens towards the posterior end.

➢ There is a cardiac or **stomodeal** valve at the end of the fore-gut that retains the chewed mulberry leaf bits in the oesophagus for sometime and also prevents the regurgitation of food from mid-gut to fore-gut.

➢ The mid-gut is a long, wide, cylindrical tube narrow at the posterior end. Digestion and assimilation of food take place mainly in the mid-gut. The **digestive fluid** is secreted principally from the **goblet cells** at the **mid-gut** epithelium and the cylindrical cells absorb the digested food.

➢ The fore and hind guts have a chitinous lining, but an inner layer of **peritropic membrane** in the mid-gut generally protects the mid-gut epithelium from mechanical damage due to food particles.

➢ The hind gut consists of the **small intestine**, colon and rectum, and a pylorus valve near the anterior end of the small intestine which guards and regulates the passage of digested food from the mid-gut to the hind-gut.

- The hind-gut is a passage for the absorption of a larger portion of food moisture and elimination of digested food. In the anterio-posterior direction the rectum has six muscles for pressing the excrements.
- The faecal matter is pressed in the rectum and expelled from the anus as faecal pellets bearing **hexagonal marks.**
- In the adult the **proboscis** is **vestigial** as well as non-functional and the adult does not feed. Hence the adult digestive system appears **degenerated** and **less prominent** than the larval digestive system.

- ❖ **Silk glands**

- Silk glands are transformed **labial glands**, ectodermal in origin, cylindrical and tubular. They are situated on the ventro-lateral sides of the mid intestine and the posterior ends are blind.
- Anteriorly, the paired ducts unite and open into the '**spinneret'**. Silk glands may be divided into three distinct regions; **anterior**, **middle** and **posterior**.
- The anterior region is a straight tube opening at the fore end into the duct and posteriorly into the middle region.
- The **middle region** is the **largest** of the three regions and has three definite flexions. The middle region is again divided into three functionally different sections; **anterior**, **middle** and **posterior**.
- A pair of glands known as **Filippi's or Lyonnet's glands** is situated at the junction of the two anterior regions. A viscous fluid is secreted by these glands and their exact function is not clear.
- **Fibroin**, the silk protein, is secreted from the **posterior region**. The **middle region** acts as a reservoir for the **maturation** of fibroin and also secretes sericin around the **fibroin** as below.
- **Sericin I,** the innermost sericin, is secreted from the posterior section of the **middle region**; **Sericin II,** the middle layered sericin, from the **middle section** of the middle region; **Sericin III,** outermost sericin from the **anterior** section of the **middle** region.
- The **anterior** region of the silk gland **does not secrete** any particular substance; it is simply a **passage** and carries the silk substance from the **reservoir** (middle region) for freezing.

- The threads of the two sides are called '**brins**' and the sericin layer of the two bind them together into a single filament or '**bave**'.
- The ripe silkworm moves its head in a figure of **eight** pattern during the process of cocoon **spinning**. As soon as the liquid silk comes out from the spinneret through its orifice, it is fixed to the surface of the **mountage** by sericin.
- The combined force of both drawing and ejection which acts on the aqueous silk results in the spinning of the thread. The spinning rate of the silkworm is **360 – 480 mm / min**.
- The **water content** of the silk fibre at the spinneret is about **70%.** When the silk fibre comes out of the spinneret and comes into contact with air, the water evaporates immediately from the fibre and many pores are formed in the fibre.

- ❖ **Excretory system**
- The **Malpighian tubes** are the primary organs of **excretion**. In the larva, the Malpighian tubes arise at the junction of small intestine and colon in the hind gut of the digestive tract.
- The tube arising on each side of the hind gut is enlarged into an excretory chamber from which two branches arise. One of the tubes situated on the dorsal side branches further into three tubes.
- In all, there are **three pairs** of **Malpighian tubes** in the silkworm larva that stick to the mid gut and run towards the anterior side, turn back and ultimately open into the rectum.
- Nitrogenous compounds like protein are metabolized by these tubes and excreted principally as **uric acid**. They also excrete **calcium oxalate**. The Malpighian tubes in the mature larva are **light yellow** and they contain large quantities of **yellow vitamin B2**.

- ❖ **Silkworm races**
- Voltinism refers to the number of broods raised per year. It is a genetically determined character which exerts its effect through hormones. Based on voltinism, three kinds of races are recognized in mulberry silkworm, Univoltines, bivoltines and multivoltines.

Characteristic feature	Uni / Bivoltine	Multivoltine
Egg	Diapausing / Non-diapausing	Non - diapausing

Length of silk filament in cocoon (m)	1000 – 1600	300 -400
Shell ratio (%)	15 -25	10 -12

❖ **Different races of silk worm**

Multivoltine Races	1. Multivoltines or polyvoltines have more than **three generations** per year. 2. The larval duration is **short**. Larvae are **resistant** to **high temperature** and **high humidity.** 3. They are well adapted to **tropical** conditions where mulberry sprouts throughout the year. 4. Larvae and cocoon are small in size. Commercially these cocoons are **poor quality**. 5. The adults lay **non-diapausing** eggs. **Multivoltine** races of tropical region generally produce **coloured cocoons** – greenish or golden-yellow.
Bivoltine Races	1. **Bivoltine** races have **two generations** per year, the first-generation adults developing from eggs hatched in spring lay non-diapausing eggs. 2. The **second-generation** adults developing from these eggs lay eggs which remain **dormant** till next spring. 3. The larval duration is longer as that of **univoltines**. Larvae are robust and tolerate environmental fluctuations they are used for summer and autumn rearing in temperate regions. 4. By careful manipulation of **artificial breaking** and **incubation,** a third crop can be raised using late summer and early autumn leaves. 5. The **bivoltine** cocoons are commercially **superior. Japanese** and **Chinese** races have both **uni** and **bivoltine** varieties

❖ **Multivoltine Silk worm Races**

C. Nichi	This was originally a **Japanese** bivoltine race which was imported and introduced in the state of **Mysore**. Due to continuous rearing by seed producers, this race has now **degenerated** to a **multivoltine** race
Nistari	This is one of the indigenous multivoltine races which is continuously being reared not only for producing cross breed hybrids, but also as a **commercial indigenous** race. It was introduced in **1881** from **China** and continues to dominate commercial rearing in the entire North India, especially in West Bengal.
Pure Mysore	It was imported from **China** in 1895. The main **demerit** of this race is its **long larval period** (about 27-28 days).
Sarupat	This race belongs to the **North – Eastern** part of India.
Tamil Nadu white	Some **multivoltine** races of India are able to produce white cocoons. Tamil Nadu Sericulture Department isolated the race called TNW in 1975.

❖ **Bivoltine races**

Races developed by CSR & TI, Mysore	NB 7, NB 18, NB 4 D2, CSR 2, CSR 3, CSR 4, CSR 5, CSR 6, CSR 12, CSR 16, CSR 17, CSR 18 , CSR 19
Races developed by RSRS, Kalimpong	KA (Kalimpong)
Races developed by KSSRDI, Bangalore	KSO 1 and SP 2

❖ **Silkworm Hybrids**

CSR2 × CSR4	1. Year of recommendation: **1997,**

	2. Productive **bivoltine hybrid** Plain larvae with bluish white body colour 3. Larval period: **23-24 days** 4. Bright white hybrid shaped cocoons with medium grains 5. Cocoon yield: **65-70 kg /100 dfls** 6. Pupation rate: **>90 %** 7. Raw silk: **17-18 %** 8. Reelability: **86-90 %** 9. Filament length: **1000 m** 10. Fibre quality: **2A-3A** 11. Renditta: **5.5-6.0** 12. Better crop stability with commercial farmers
CSR16 × CSR17	1. Productive **bivoltine hybrid** Marked larvae with bluish white body colour 2. Larval period: **23-24 days** 3. Bright white hybrid shaped cocoons with medium grains 4. Cocoon yield: **65-70 kg /100 dfls** 5. Pupation rate: **>90 %** 6. Raw silk: **18-19 %** 7. Reelability: **86-90 %** 8. Filament length: **1050 m** 9. Fibre quality: **2A-3A** 10. Renditta: **5.5-6.0** 11. Alternative to **CSR2 × CSR4**
FC1 × FC2 (CSR6 × CSR26) × (CSR2 × CSR27)	Productive **bivoltine double** hybrid (**2000**)
Chamaraja (CSR50 × CSR51)	Robust **bivoltine** hybrid (2012)

Jayachamaraja (CSR50 × CSR52) × (CSR51 × CSR53)	Productive **bivoltine double hybrid** (2012)
G11 × G19	**Double hybrid** for sub-optimal conditions (2014)
S8 × CSR16	Productive **bivoltine hybrid** (2015)
PM × CSR2	Productive **multi x bivoltine** (2000)
Cauvery Gold (MV1 × S8)	Productive improved cross breed **tolerant to silkworm diseases (2015)**

❖ **Silkworm rearing**

➢ **Disinfection:** It is defined as the process of destruction or inactivation of harmful micro-organism in water either by physical process or chemical process. One of the major reasons for crop losses in cocoon production is the diseases of silkworms.

Physical disinfection	1. **Sun drying:** This consists of exposing the rearing applieances to direct sunlight for disinfection. Sunlight is used mainly for disinfection of wooden rearing trays. The bactericidal effect of sun light that kill pathogens by denaturation of their proteins. The action U.V light is supplemented by infrared rays. It is cheap and considered as effective method. 2. **By boiling water:** Boiling water destroys the pathogens by coagulation of their proteins. This is simple but found effective for small rearing tools, nets, chopsticks and brushes. These are put into boiling water for 30 min, dried and used. 3. **By steam:** Steam at high pressure denatures the proteins of pathogens and it is considered as a good sterilizing agent.

	4. **By hot air:** This is a good sterilizing method in which hot air is turned into the room containing the appliances to be sterilized
Chemical disinfection	1. Formalin: Formalin is a solution of **formaldehyde gas** in water. It is a colourless, transparent and neutral liquid with a pungent irritating odour. Its disinfection power is due to its **reducing action** on the protoplasm of germs by removing oxygen from the and becoming converted to formic acid. a) **2%** for **routine** disinfection b) **5%** for rearing room and appliance after **pebrine infction** c) **0.7-0.8% formaline** is sprayed directly on the worms during **muscardine** infection 2. **Bleaching powder** solution Bleaching powder, also called **chlorkalk**, is a powder containing **calcium hydroxide, calcium chloride and calcium hypochlorite** with an irritating odour. Its disinfection action is an **oxidation** reaction due to the evolution of nascent oxygen which **oxidizes** the **germs** and kills them. 3. **Formaldehyde gas** This gas has a strong irritating odour, a weak penetrating powder and is colourless. The doors and windows are closed airtight before fumigating and kept closed for 24 hours . Then the room and tools are washed with water and dried. 4. **Sodium hypochlorite** It is non-toxic, pale yellow solution with unpleasant smell and strong bleaching action. Soluble in water and can be used safely. It is generally used for disinfection of rearing room and equipment.

❖ **Bed disinfection:** Bed disinfectants are used to prevent germs released by diseased worms or entering through contamination. These bed disinfectants are employed in different stages of rearing.

Lime powder	Lime powder and **ceresan lime** are widely used in many countries like China, Japan and India. They are cheap, readily available and have a strong disinfecting effect on many pathogens causing diseases.
Formalinised chaff	The chaff is soaked in **0.6% formalin** during for young-age worms and **0.8% formalin** for late-age worms.
Kanavectine	This is special larval disinfection developed by USRI, **Ukraine** as a **bed disinfectant**. Application of this on the 2nd and 3rd day of fifth instar minimizes bacterial disease of about **20%**.
Resham Keet Oushadh	RKO developed by CSR&TI, Mysore, Karnataka, is a dust formulation used as a bed disinfectant to prevent **grasserie** and **muscardine**. It is a mixture of **benzoic acid, paraformaldehyde and lime**. It is recommended that the formulation be dusted on worms through a thin muslin cloth once, after moult and before initiation of the first feeding at the rate of **3g ft^2** for I-III instar **5 g ft^2** for the fourth and fifth instars.
Resham Jyothi	This is effective bed disinfectant dusted over the silkworms in the rearing bed. This formulation is non-pungent and effective against **graserie, bacterial flacherie, muscardine, IFV, DNV** and **pebrine** feeding should be resumed after 30 min.
Sanjeevini	This bed disinfectant is very popular among farmers of southern India as **'A' powder**, was formulated by **KSSRDI**, Bangalore. Unlike other **bed disinfectants**, it is being used on the rearing trays prior to brushing and also on newly hatched worms.

Vijetha	This product was developed by the **CST&RI, Mysore**. This is a silkworm body and rearing seat disinfectant of unique formulation effective against all silkworm diseases. At the rate of three kg **vijetha** are required for dusting silkworm of **100 dfls.**
Labex	It is a slightly different formulation, used as an **anti muscardine** and anti **grasserie** bed disinfectant. It is applied once in each instar upto IV and daily once in V instar at the rate of 4 g per 0.1 m^2.
Amruth	An eco-friendly plant-based formulation for suppressing **Grasserie** and **Flacherie**.
Ankush	This is an **eco-friendly** bed disinfectant that prevents the spread of common silkworm diseases
Moncozeb	It is mixed with dust and spread over worms. It is not only helps in keeping the bed dry, but also protects freshly ecdysoid worms from fungal infection. For chawki worms once after moult at a concentration of 0.8% moncozeb mixed with lime powder and 1, 2 and 3 g per sq ft for the 1st, 2nd and 3rd instars respectively.
Paffsol	**Paffsol** and **5% calcium selenate** are used as bed disinfectants. In the case of just hatched larvae, 1.5g disinfectant is applied for an area of 0.1 m^2. Thereafter, at every stage of the larvae 5 g per 0.1m^2 area is sprayed.
Serifit	**Serifit** (Chlorine based product) was developed by CSRTI, Mysuru and M/s SreeRayalaseema Hi-Strength Hypo Ltd, Kurnool, Andhra Pradesh
Sanitech/Serichlor (Chlorine dioxide) 1996	Disinfection of rearing houses, surroundings and appliances. For maintenance of personal and rearing hygiene

Asthra (CSRTI, 2009)	A general disinfectant for Sericulture. Effective against all silkworm pathogens at 0.05% concentration. Easy to prepare and spray

❖ Environmental requirements for different stages of silkworm

Temperature	1. **I instar** - 26 -28°C 2. **II instar** - 26 -28°C 3. **III instar** - 25 – 26°C 4. **IV instar** - 24 – 26°C 5. **V instar** - 24 – 25 °C
Humidity	1. **I instar** - 85% RH 2. **II instar** - 85% RH 3. **III instar** - 80% RH 4. **IV instar** - 75% RH 5. **V instar** - 70% RH
Aeration	1.Unwanted gases have to be replaced by fresh air containing more oxygen for the healthy growth of the silkworms.
Light	1. Dim light of **20-30 lux** 2. Uniform throughout **(16 hours a day)** and darkness **(8 hours a day)**

❖ Incubation

➢ Incubation is the process of preserving silkworm eggs under optimum environmental condition for ensuring hatching percentage. The optimum environmental conditions are as follows

Temperature	25°C ± 1°C

Relative humidity	70 to 80%,
Photoperiod	16 hr of light 8 hrs darkness 15-20 lux light intensity
Air current	0.3m per sec

- ➢ Incubation of eggs begins from the day of oviposition. Normally **10 days** are required from egg laying to hatching, which however may vary from **9 to 11 days** according to temperature and humidity. In case of preserved eggs, the incubation time is 7-9 days only.
- ➢ Incubation at **25°C temperature, 80% relative humidity** and **16 hours of light** per day is ideal for silkworm eggs.
- ➢ Wet foam strips may be used whenever Relative humidity falls **below 70%.**
- ➢ **16 hours light and 8 hours** dark is ideal for incubation particularly in bivoltine eggs.
- ➢ **Methods of incubation**

Constant temperature incubation	1. In constant temperature incubation is carried out till hatching at a constant temperature of **23- 26°C (23 °C for univoltine** and **26 °C for bivoltine and multivoltine**). 2. **Non hibernating** and acid treated eggs are incubated by this method. 3. Cold stored eggs either or before acid treatment must be subjected to an intermediate temperature of **15°C** for a few hours before being incubated
Raised temperature incubation	In raised temperature Incubation method is used for incubating **hibernating eggs**, in this method soon after the release of eggs from cold storage they are preserved at 1. 10-15°C for 3days, 2. 18-20°C for 2days, 3. 23-24°C for 4days 4. 25-26°C till hatching.

❖ **Black Boxing**

➢ Before **48 hours** of hatching a black spot appears on the egg. This condition is referred as **'Head Pigmentation'** stage.

➢ One day before **hatching (24 hours before)**, the eggs turn black or blue in colour. This is referred as body pigmentation stage or **"blue eggs"** satge.

➢ The silkworm eggs in the body pigmentation stage are artificially confined to a dark phase or **'Scotophase'** prior to hatching and the process is referred to as **Black Boxing of Eggs.**

➢ **Reason for doing black boxing:** Development of eggs is observed faster in light than in darkness till head pigmentation stage. From the head pigmentation stage, conversely, darkness expedites the developmental process. By exploiting this developmental process, the early maturing embryo is prevented from hatching and the late embryos are given time to develop and catch up with the early maturing worms. The next day they are exposed suddenly to diffused light so that the larvae hatch out most uniformly responding to the phototropic stimulus. By this method hatching percentage of 90 and above is attained.

❖ **Hatching**

➢ The newly developed larvae breaks out the eggs shell and comes out and is called **hatching**. The hatched larvae are **brushed** and **reared**. The newly hatched larvae are black, hairy and look like small ants and are called **"ants"** or **"kengo"**

➢ Hatching Percentage: The ratio between hatched eggs and total no. of eggs in a laying is called **"hatching percentage"**.

Hatching percentage= (Total No.of eggs hatched/ Total No.of eggs) X 100

❖ **Brushing**

➢ When the eggs hatch, the emerged larvae are to be collected for rearing. This process of separating kego /ants from egg sheet or egg shell is called "brushing".

➢ **Methods of brushing**

Brushing of loose eggs	The eggs are spread evenly in one layer in the egg box and kept in black box at blue egg stage. On the next day when all eggs reach blue egg stage they are removed from black box and covered with a thin perforated cloth or a fine mesh or finely perforated paper. This covering is placed in such a way that it just touches the upper surface of the eggs. Then just before brushing, chopped mulberry leaves are sprinkled on the top of the net or cloth or paper. This mulberry leaf attracts the hatched worms to crawl on to the upper surface. When maximum number of worms hatches out and crawls on to the paper they are transferred to rearing tray.
Brushing of egg cards	1. Tapping method 2. Feather method 3. Brushing with mulberry leaves 4. Husk - feeding method 5. Net and feeding method of Brushing

❖ **Methods of silkworm rearing**

Chawki rearing methods	1. Paraffin paper rearing 2. Box rearing 3. Wrap up Method of Chawki Rearing 4. Co-operative rearing
Late age rearing methods	1. Shelf rearing 2. Floor rearing 3. Shoot rearing (**Most economical and most common**)

❖ **Feeding**

➢ The quality of the cocoon harvested depends mainly on the quality of leaves fed during rearing. Feeding must satisfy both the appetite of the larvae and its nutritional requirement.

- Chawki worms require tender, soft and succulent leaves with around 80% moisture and high nutritive value. Mulberry leaves having **27% protein**, **11% carbohydrates**, **minerals** and **vitamins** are considered good for rearing.

- The late age silkworms require relatively less moisture in leaves, but the leaves should be nutritious. Leaves from 55 - 65 days old shoots are ideal. Over-mature leaves, above 70 days old and tender leaves less than 35 days old should be avoided for late age silkworms.

- **Nutrid – Semi-synthetic diet for rearing young age silkworms:** The diet allows **Chawki** rearers to rear **multi x bivoltine** hybrids of their choice on semi-synthetic diet up to **II moult.** A **nutritive** and **hygienic** alternative that reduces infections in the early larval stages.

- **Quantity of feeding**

Multivoltine x Bivoltine HYBRID	708-750 kg/100 dfl
Bivoltine x bivoltine	850-907 kg/100 dfl

❖ **Bed cleaning**

- It is a process to remove waste and harmful material found in the rearing bed.

- **Frequency of Cleaning**

I Instar	Once
II instar	Twice i.e., one just after the 1st moult and again before setting for 2nd moult.
III instar	Thrice i.e., once after moult, once in the middle of 3rd age and once just before setting for 4th moult.
IV and V instars	Daily

- **Method of Cleaning**
    1. Cleaning with husk
    2. Cleaning with Net.
    3. Cleaning with husk and net

❖ **Moulting (Ecdysis)**

➢ Periodical process of shedding the old cuticle accompanied by the formation of new cuticle is known as **moulting** or **ecdysis**. It is a sensitive period lasting for **15-30 hrs**.

➢ The cuticular parts discarded during moulting is known as **exuvia**. Moulting occurs many times in an insect during the immatured stages before attaining the adult-hood.

➢ The time interval between the two subsequent moulting is called as **stadium** and the form assumed by the insect in any **stadium** is called as **instar**.

1st instar	3 to 3 ½ days	I moult
2nd instar	2 ½ to 3 days	II moult
3rd instar	3 to 3 ½ days	III moult
4th instar	4 to 4 ½ days	IV moult
5th instar	6 to 7 days	Spinning
Total	**23-26 days**	

➢ **Moulting** is controlled by endocrine glands like prothoracic gland which secrete moulting hormone. Endocrine glands are activated by **prothoracico-tropic** hormones produced by neurosecretory cells of brain.

Characteristics before moult	1. Worms about to moult have a stout and shiny body 2. Dark small sized head 3. Worms move to the periphery of the bed
Characteristics during moult	1. Moulting worms stops feeding 2. Holds its body vertically **3.** Wriggles out of its old skin
Characteristics after moult	1. Newly moulted worms have a larger head 2. Loose and less shiny skin **3.** Worms have more appetite

➢ **Care during moult**

1. The moulting duration is longer in 4th moult as compared to that in other moults (1-3).

2. Under optimum conditions of temperature (24 degree C) and humidity (60-70%). it occupies about 30 hrs.

3. When larvae show moulting symptoms, rearing bed is spread as to make a uniform thin layer to facilitate quick drying of leaf over mulberry leaves and to reduce the humidity in the bed.

4. Whenever the humidity of rearing house is more, a thin layer of lime should be dusted on the rearing bed to render the excess moisture to be absorbed which helps in smooth moulting process.

➢ **Silkworm behaviour during maturity**

1. On the sixth or seventh day of fifth instar, the silkworms show less appetite and discharge hard dark brown coloured faeces which are soon replaced by soft light brown ones, which indicate that spinning stage has set in.

2. The skin becomes gradually transparent due to growth of silk gland which occupies almost the whole body, when the entire gut remains emptied.

3. Silkworm discharge liquid excreta at the time of cocooning. Hence, it is necessary that good ventilation is provided in the mounting room to drive away moisture.

4. The body shrinks in length and there is a visible constriction at the 4th and 5th segments.

5. The worm stops feeding and moves towards edge of the place to make a cocoon by spitting out the liquid silk through spinneret located below the mouth.

6. Silk material is secreted and immediately fixed and hardened when silkworm touch spinneret to any solid matter.

7. When silkworm moves, the silk materials are drawn out from the spinneret to the point where the spinneret touches next. A silkworm can spin silk filament length ranging from 500 m to 1500 m depending on the breed

➢ **Sampoorna- a hormone for uniform maturity of silkworm**

1. Sampoorna is a **plant-based steroid** with **moulting hormone**

2. Sampoorna can be used for early and uniform maturation of larvae. It saves labour in picking the matured worms.

3. Usually, the process of silkworm maturation lasts for **24-48** hours and in winter season, it may extend further.

4. Farmers, therefore have to pick the ripe worms continuously there by incurring additional expenditure.

5. To overcome this, a plant-based hormone **Sampoorna** has been developed and spraying this hormone on the leaves given during sample spinning stage, hastens the maturation of all worms uniformly within 18-24 days of the spray.

❖ **Spinning**

➢ Soon after moulting the mature larva passes out its last excreta in a **semi solid condition**. This differs from the normal faeces in colour and often has a **reddish** band and is referred to as **red faeces**.

➢ It contains a large amount of **uric acid** and colour is due to **tryptophan** metabolites. After emptying its gut, it first secretes a tiny droplet of silk which harden and sticks on the mountage.

➢ This is its **anchorage spot**. The worm anchors itself by this fluid. It first spins a loose **hammock** forming the framework of the cocoon. This layer called **blaze or floss (Outermost layer)**, through formed of continuous filament is a tangled mass and is unreelable.

➢ In **univoltine** and bivoltine floss layer forms only **2%** by weight of the entire cocoon but in the **multivoltine** it forms nearly **10%**.

➢ After getting good foot hold in the **hammock** the larva lays down the cocoon in compact layers. Due to the characteristic movement of the head during spinning, the filament is spun in the shape of **S or ∞.** The former type is common in the outer layer of the cocoon shell and the latter type usual in the middle and inner layer.

➢ After the compact shell is formed the larva shrinks and covers itself with a gossamer or thin layer of silk. It detaches itself from the shell moults and becomes transformed into pupa. The last layer of thin silk is called the **pelade layer (Inner most layer)** of the cocoon and is **unreelable**.

➢ **Samruddhi (JHA Technology)** for enhanced cocoon/silk production: Increases cocoon and shell weight by **12-15%** with no adverse effect on shell percentage.

❖ **Mounting**

- The process of **transferring matured** larvae to a suitable frame to spin cocoon is called **mounting**.
- After mounting, larva takes **48 hours** for complete spinning of cocoon depending on the environmental conditions.
- Hence, protection of larvae for 3-4 days after mounting has a profound influence on quality of cocoons. Hence, in a mass rearing when 40% of the larvae show maturation, all the larvae can be collected and mounted at the same time.
- **25°C temperature, 60-65% humidity,** good ventilation and uniform light are necessary in the mounting room for obtaining good quality cocoons.
- Mount only matured larvae. Mounting of un-ripened or over mature larvae results in defective and inferior quality cocoons.

- **Methods of Mounting**
    1. Picking – up for Mounting
    2. By shaking the shoots
    3. **Jobrai Method** (Shaking of the mulberry shoots containing matured silkworms)
    4. Net Method
    5. Branch Method
    6. Self – Mounting

- **Types of Mountages**

Bamboo chandrike	1. It is the most **commonly used** mountage in India.
	2. It is made of bamboo spirals woven on a bamboo mat with two supporting bamboo sticks. The mat is of size **1.8 x 1.2 m.**
	3. Matured silkworms are transferred to the chandrike @ **40-50 worms** per sq ft.
	4. After mounting, the chandrike is kept at a slanting back position of **45°** to allow the urine to fall on the ground and to prevent the staining of cocoons.

Plastic collapsible mountage	1. These are also called as **Netrikes** and are made of plastic mesh having 11 folds of 2.2" height and can be placed in a wooden tray of size 2' x 3' for mounting the larvae. 2. Each mountage can hold **350-400** larvae for spinning.
Rotary cardboard mountage	1. These are made of pieces of cardboard assembled in a checkered pattern consisting of **13 rows and 12 sections** each providing a total mounting space of 156 sections of size 4.5 x 3 x 3 cm. 2. Each frame can hold **1,560 larvae** for spinning, but only 80 % is allowed to mount, i.e., about **1,300 larvae** to provide sufficient spacing.
Bottlebrush mountage	1. Different types of bottle brush mountages are available depending on the material used, like plastic, bamboo and coconut broomstick. 2. Plastic bottle brush is a machine-made plastic material with individual pieces. Each bottle brush assembled is one meter long and can mount **350-400 larvae**.
Dried grass/straw/ twigs mountage	1. When silkworm starts maturing, a thick layer of dried grass or straw is spread over the rearing bed. 2. Matured larvae crawl through the bed on the mountage and spin cocoons. 3. For mounting **100 dfls** of larvae, **80 m2** space is required.

❖ **Cocoon harvesting**

➢ harvesting of cocoon must be done on the **6th or 7th day** after spinning. However, seed cocoons should be **harvested** on **8th day**.

➢ The silkworm larva metamorphosis into pupa after spinning the cocoons for about **48 hours** from the time they are mounted. Generally, pupation takes place on the **4th day of spinning**.

➢ Thus, the worms inside the cocoons will be still in the form of pre pupa, which has a delicate cuticular skin.

➢ Thus, if the cocoons are handled before this stage, the skin may rupture and body fluid will **ooze** and stain the cocoons, making it unsuitable for reeling. Thus, early harvesting of cocoons should be strictly avoided.

❖ **Transportation of cocoons**

➢ The cocoons should be put into loosely woven cotton bags each weighing about **10kg.** They are loosely packed and transported in **cooler hours** of the day (i.e., **morning or evening**).

❖ **Deflossing**

➢ Removing of the flossy layer from the cocoon is called **Deflossing**.

➢ **Deflossing** is a pre-requisite for extraction of silk (Reeling). During the process of reeling, floss is removed by brushing. In this process, some portion of reelable silk also goes as waste.

❖ **Sorting of cocoons**

➢ Removal of **odd shaped** and **defective cocoons** from the lots is called sorting of cocoons.

➢ Defective cocoons affect the **reeling performance** and quality of the silk.

➢ Therefore, unsuitable cocoons are to be sorted out from the good cocoons to get optimum result during reeling.

❖ **Classification of defective cocoons**

Double cocoons	1. A double cocoon is spun by two worms, producing a filament, which does not unwind smoothly and tangles easily. 2. Silk extracted from this is known as "**Dupion silk**"
Inside stained cocoons (dead cocoons)	1. Dead cocoons are also known as **melted cocoons**. In this case, the pupa is dead and sticks to the inside shell of the cocoon causing a stain. **2.** Melted cocoons are called **mutes** because they do not make a sound when shaken.
Outside stained cocoons (dead cocoons)	1. These are recognized by a rusty colour spot on the cocoon shell caused by absorption of intestinal fluid/urine of the mature worm formed during moulting. **2. Reelability** is very poor in this case.
Mountage pressed cocoons	1. This defect may happen due to improper mounting frames. **2.** These are also called scaffold pressed cocoons.
Deformed cocoons	1. This defect may happen due to improper mounting frames. **2.** These are also called **scaffold pressed cocoons.**
Flimsy cocoons	1. The shell is loosely spun in layers and has a low silk content. **2.** These cocoons are easily **overcooked** and produce waste.

Thin-end cocoons	1. One or both ends of the cocoon are very thin and there is a risk of bursting when processed. 2. The cause of this defect may be attributed to racial characteristics or improper temperature and humidity during rearing and mounting.
Multi layered cocoons	1. Cocoons having two are three layered shells. 2. The cause of this defect may be attributed to racial characteristics
Pierced cocoons	1. This happens when a moth has emerged or in the case of the emergence of **uzifly**. 2. Pierced cocoons are unfit for reeling and can be used only for hand spinning or as raw material of machine spun silk yarn.

❖ **Assessment of cocoons quality**

Cocoon Weight	Cocoons are being **sold** on **weight basis**. You will find that the weight of the cocoons gradually decreases due to moisture loss and consumption of the fat till the **pupa** transform into moth and emerge out.
Assessment of Cocoons for Defective cocoon Percentage	If the lot is not sorted properly, you can assess percentage of defective cocoons in a lot. For this, take one kg of cocoon from the lot at random. Sort out defective cocoons like double, flimsy, melted, pierced etc. Count and weigh good and defective cocoons separately.
Rendita	It represents the quantity of green (fresh) cocoons required to produce **1 kg**. of raw silk. If 10 kg. of green (fresh) cocoon of a lot is required to produce 1 kg raw silk, then **Rendita** of that lot is 10. It is an **indicator** of price fixation of the cocoon when purchased for reeling.

Shell ratio (%)	It indicates the quantity of silk shell in terms of cocoon weight and expressed in percentage. This value gives a clear indication of quantity of raw silk that can be reeled from a lot of fresh cocoons. It is used for estimating **Rendita** and ultimately helps in price fixation. **Formula = (Weight of shell/weight of cocoon) x 100**

❖ **Important technologies**

DFL	Disease free layings. 1 DFL- 400eggs.
Mounting	The transfer of ripened larvae to cocoonages
Brushing	The transfer of newly hatched larvae to rearing sheets
Stiffling	Post-harvest process of killing pupae inside cocoons by Hot air / Steam /Sun drying
Riddling	sorting of coccons
Renditta	No. of kg of coccons required to produce 1kg of silk
Denier	<ul><li>Weight of 9000m of silk thread. (1.7-2.8g)</li><li>Denier is the measure of thickness of silk. International standard – 14 deniers</li></ul>
Grainage	The place where silkworm eggs are produced.
Filature	Large factory where cocoons are reeled to produce silk.
Skein	<ul><li>Silk having a diameter of 1.5m and weighs 70g.(20-22deniers)</li><li>Group of skeins produce Book (2kg). Group of books form Bale.</li><li>Indian bale – 50kgs & International Bale – 60kgs.</li></ul>
Shell ratio	wt of cocoon shell/ wt of cocoon ×100
Reelability	% of broken filament / % of whole filament
Arboriculture	Planting of trees for rearing silkworm other than *B.mori*

❖ **Diseases of Silkworms**

Pebrine disease/Pepper disease/Corpuscle disease	1. Caused by Protozoa (*Nosema bombycis*). 2. All stages are infected. Transmitted through eggs. (Transovarial transmission) 3. **Symptoms**: **Eggs** are laid in clumps. **Larvae** with wrinkled skin, poor appetite. **Adults** – wings scaleless at spots, unstretched wings & swollen abdomen
Flacherie/ sappe / thatte disease	1. Caused by *Bt.* var.sotto. 2. Mode of infection: spores & due to bad rearing conditions. **3.** Symptoms: Putrefied larvae, diarrohea.
Grasserie/ Halthonde	1. Caused by Borellina virus. 2. Symptoms: swelling of segments, flimpsy cocoons. **3.** Larvae appears like a Bomboo cane
Muscardine	1. Common in humid places. 2. White M– *Beauvaria bassiana* 3. Green M– *Spicaria prasina.* 4. Yellow M- *Iscaria farinose* 5. Larvae about to spin cocoon is susceptible to this disease. 6. Oil-soaked lesions on the larvae. **7.** Management: Cerasen lime or Dithane M-45 is spread on the bed in a thin layer

❖ **Pests of Silkworms**

Uzifly: *Exorista sorbillans* F: Tachinidae, *Tricholyga bombycis*	1. 1 st reported in Japan -1917 2. Endoparasitic on larvae, blackspot at the point of entry.

	3. Comes & pupates in the soil.
	4. Lays 1-2eggs/larvae of 4th & 5th instar
	5. Management:
	Uzitrap, uzicide, uzitablet.
	Ectopupal parasitoid: *Nesolynx thymus* (Eulopidae)
Beetles: (*Dermestes ater, Dermestis cadaverensis*)	1. Eat eggs & pupa.
Earwig	*Labia arachidis*

❖ **Non-mulberry silkworms**

Eri silkworm (*Samia cynthia ricini*), F: Saturnidae	2. **Semidomesticated** in nature.
	3. Main Hosts:
	Castor –*Ricinus communis*
	Kasseru- *Hetereopanyx fragrans*
	Other hosts:
	Tapioca- *Manihot utillisima*
	Payam- *Evodia flaxinifolia*
	Papaya – *Carica papaya*
	4. Multivoltine in nature.
	5. Produces open ended coccons, which can't be reeled.
	6. Produce Brick red colored silk, not as glossary as mulberry silk.
	7. Called as **Poorman's silk / Arandi silk.** Silk is not a single strand here.
Tropical Tasar silkworm (*Antharaea mylitta*), F: Saturniidae	1. Temperate Tasar silkworm species:
	A.yamamai in **Japan**
	A.roylei in **India**
	A.pernyi in **china**.
	2. Wild in nature, not domesticated.

	3. **Bivoltine**.
	4. Silk press is narrow constriction near spinneret, silk is passed through it to form fine silk thread present only in Tasar SW.
	5. Main hosts: *Terminalia tomentosus* & *Terminalia arjuna*
	6. Other hosts: Saal- *Shorea robusta* Ber – *Zizyphus jujuba*
	7. Cocoons are large with a **peduncle**.
	8. **Pupal diapause** is seen.
	9. **Mauni/Monia**: palm leaf vessels used for mating
	10. Tasar uzifly – *Belpharipa zepina*
Muga silkworm (*Antharaea assamensis*)	1. Semidomesticated in nature, Native to **Assam**.
	2. **Multivoltine**.
	3. Hosts: **Som-** *Machilus bombycina* **Soalu** – *Litsea polyantha*
	4. Silk is called as Mejenkori silk, golden yellow color.
	5. Eggs are laid in dried leaves called **Kharika**.
	6. The cocoonages are called **Jali**.
	7. The reeling machine is called **Bhir**.
	8. Peak day of harvest is called **Bharpok**

❖ **Important points of sericulture**

1. Silkworm was discovered during **2640 BC**

2. Usefulness of silk given by **Lotzu**.

3. Silk glands are modified salivary glands. i.e **Labial glands.**

4. Silk is produced from spinneret, which opens on anterior margin of labium.

5. Silk contains 3 types of proteins:

    a. Fibroin – Elastic protein -75% **(Glycine, Alanine & Tyrosine)**

    b. Sericin – Gum protein – 25% **(Serine, Alanine & leucine)**

    c. Outer floss.

6. **Fibroin** is produced from **posterior part** of silk glands.

7. **Sericin** is produced in **middle part** of silk glands.

8. Silk is **stored** in **middle** of the anterior part of silk gland

9. Silk produced by **univoltine** race is of **superior quality.**

10. **1 kg of silk** is produced from **7-8kg** of cocoons.

11. **1kg of silk** is produced from **120-160kg** of mulberry leaves.

12. Weight of a cocoon is **1.67g.**

13. **Ishiwata's gland** on **8th & 9th** abd.segments in female.

14. **Herold's gland** b/w **8th & 9th** abd.segments in male.

15. **Female pupa** has **X-mark** on 8th and.segment & **male pupa** has a **dot.**

16. Employment potential of Indian Silk industry is **85 lakhs**

17. Central Silk Institute for Muga and Eri research is located at **Ladoigharh, Assam**

18. Silk gained entry to India through **Tibet**

19. Major consumer of silk in the world is **India**

20. Mulberry variety recommended for shade condition is **Sahana**

21. Cultivation of Mulberry is termed as **Moriculture**

22. Biofertilizer that Fixes nitrogen in Mulberry is **Azatobacter**

23. Mulberry inflorescence is called **Catkin**

24. Most suitable soil type for mulberry is **Red loamy Soil**

25. Mulberry plant is **Highly cross pollinated**

26. Manophagus nature of mulberry leaf is due to the biting factor **Morin**

27. Basically, Mulberry is **Tree**

28. Perinneial natured Mulberry plant has **Taproot system**

29. Farm yard manure recommended per hectare of mulberry per year is **20 tonnes**

30. Papaya Mealy Bug menace in mulberry can be managed by release of predator *Acerophagus papaye*

31. Release of Bio-agent recommended for management of leaf roller in mulberry *Trichogramma chilonis*

32. Mulberry variety recommended for mildew resistant is **MR 2**

33. Insect responsible for causing Tukra disease is **Mealy bug**

34. Typical symptom of Bihar Hairy Caterpiller (*Spilosoma obliqu*a) infestation is **Leaf skeletonization**

35. A broad-spectrum Predator recommended For effective management of Thrips *Chrysoperla* **spp.**

36. Plant based formulation for Root knot management is **Nemahari**

37. *Diaphania pulverulentalis*- leaf roller damge in mulberry is usually seen in **Top leaves**

38. Root rot disease in mulberry is caused by **Fungi**

39. Recently recommended multi nutrient foliar spray for improving mulberry leaf quality by CSRTI, Mysore is **Poshan**

40. Management of Tukra can be effectively done through release of Both *Cryptolaemus montrouzieri* & *Scymnus coccivora*

41. Number of ovarioles in *Bombyx mori* adult are **8**

42. Number of pairs of abdominal legs in *Bomyx mori* are **5**

43. Silkworm has **9** pair of spiracles as respiratory openings

44. Mouth parts in silkworms are **Hypognathus**

45. Dorsal caudal horn in silkworm body is found on **Dorso median line of 8th abdominal segment**

46. Silk gland is modified from **Labial gland**

47. Serious pest of mulberry which is commercially exploited is ***Bombyx mori***

48. Silkworm *Bombyx mori* has **Secondary hair** type of setae on its body

49. Pupa of *Bombyx mori* is **Obtect**

50. In producing double hybrids, FC refers to **Foundation Cross**

51. CSR-2 is a popular **Bivoltine breed**

52. In silkworm rearing micro climate is monitored using **Thermohygrometer**

53. Botanical based silkworm bed disinfectant is **Ankush**

54. Optimum temperature & Relative Humidity required for chawki/young silkworms are **26-28^{0}C & 85-90%**

55. Double cocoon formation is largely due to **High density of mounting**

56. Double cross hybrids have **Four parents**

57. Orientation of Silkworm rearing house should be **East –West**

58. Marketing of Bivoltine cocoons should be done on **8th Day**

59. Number of worms mounted on chandrike / mountage per square feet **40-50**

60. Egg attains pin head stage **48hrs** before hatching.

61. In Silkworm rearing Hatching is a **Photo-periodic response**

62. Silkworms prefers more of **Dim light** for its activity

63. Rearing space required for Bivoltine Silkworm rearing is **800-900 sq.ft**

64. Hormonal formulation used for uniform maturity of silkworms is **Sampoorna**

65. In Silkworm seed production, Basic seed means **Parental seed**

66. Head quarter of National Silkworm Seed Organization is at **Bangalore**

67. In Silkworm egg production centers natural moth emergence is allowed for **Multivoltine Cocoons**

68. Preservation of male moths is done for **Second pairing**

69. Black Boxing of Silkworm eggs is done to achieve **Uniform hatching**

70. Pairing duration for Silk moths is **3-4 hours**

71. Quantity of loose eggs packed and its weight is **50 DFLs & 18 grams**

72. Mother Moth Examination is done to detect **Pebrine**

73. Silkworm Seed Technological Laboratory (SSTL) under CSB is located in **Bangalore**

74. CSR Hybrids are developed under the technical guidence of **JICA, Japan**

75. Grasserie disease in silkworms is caused by **Borrelina**

76. Calcified cocoons are the symptoms of **Fungus**

77. Ecofriendly botanical-based formulation to supress Grasserie & Flacherie is **Amruth**

78. Flacid condition in silkworms is due to combined infection of **Bacteria & virus**

79. Green muscardine disease is caused by ***Metarhizium anisoplea***

80. For effective and healthy silkworm rearing, disinfection per crop is recommended **Two times**

81. Multivoltine race resistant to diseases, used as female parent in Kolar gold Cross breed is **Pure Mysore**

82. In 1960's Sericulture vanished in France due to **Pebrine**

83. Uzi fly a major pest of silkworm, here Uzi is the name of place, where it was first noticed is in **Japan**

84. In south India Uzi fly menace was first noticed in **Karnataka**

85. Uzi fly belongs to the family **Tachinidae**

86. Uzi fly is a **Regular pest**

87. Uji maggots undergoes **3 instars**

88. *Nesolynx thymus* parasitises **Uzi pupa**

89. Uzi powder acts as a **Ovicide**

90. The grainage pest on stored cocoons is **Dermastid beetle**

91. Unit to measure the size of the cocoon is **Number/litre**

92. Single cocoon weight of bivoltine hybrids is **1.8-2.0 g.**

93. Silkworm breeds of Chinese origin spin **Oval cocoons**

94. The cocoon shell ratio of multi x bivoltine hybrids ranges from **18-20%**

95. The purpose of cocoon stifling is to **Kill pupae**

96. The quantity of cooons required to produce one kilo of raw silk is called **Renditta**

97. The extent of Fibroin in cocoon is **75-80%**

98. The shape of CSR 4 cocoon is **Dumbel**

99. Cooking of cocoon is done during silk reeling for **Softening of sericin and easy unwinding**

100. Cocoon ridling machine is used for **Grading of cocoons by size**

101. The floss content is more in the cocoons of **Pure Mysore**

102. ARM stands for **Automatic Reeling Machine**

103. Silk filament is technically known as **Bave**

104. Croissure formed during reeling ensures **Both Better Cohesion & Better tenacity**

105. The reel speed of multiend reeling machine for Bivoltine cocoons is **120 m/min**

106. The standard pH of the boiling water during reeling is **8.6**

107. Gummy component of cocoon shell is **Sericin**

108. Reelable defective cocoons are reeled on **Charaka**

109. Dupion silk is obtained from **Double cocoons**

110. Chambon type of croisure is present in **Charaka**

111. Silkwaste percent from cocoon reeling industry is **30**

112. Perimeter of Reels in Multiend reeling machine is **75 cms**

113. SCTH stands for **Silk Conditioning & Testing House**

114. Pierced cocoons are used to get **Spun silk**

115. The raw silk in the form of skein is packed as **Bale**

116. Which of the feature is the most important in quality silk reeling **Raw silk denier**

117. Central Silk Technological Research Institute is located at **Bangalore**

118. The small skein approximately should weigh **70g**

119. Evenness test is done using **Seriplane**

120. Autosorter is the machine used to measure **Size of silk**

121. Costliest silk is **Muga silk**

122. Som & Soalu are the host plants of **Muga silkworm**

123. Production of cocoonase enzyme is absent in **Eri silk moth**

124. State producing both Eri and Muga in larger quantity **Assam**

125. The Indian temperate tasar is the cross between *Antheraea pernyi X Antheraea roylei*

126. The multivoltine non-mulberry silkworm is **Eri**

127. Primary host plant of tropical tasar is *Terminalia* **spp.**

128. Central Tasar Research & Training Institue of CSB is located at **Ranchi, Jharkhand**

129. Major vanya silk produced in India is **Eri**

130. Mulberry tea is prefered for regulating **Diabetes**

131. Mulberry fruit is rich in **Vitamin C.**

132. In India Eri pupa is relished as protein rich food in **Assam**

133. Internal Sutures are made using **High quality braided silk**

134. Sericin is extracted by **High Temperature & high Pressure**

135. Fibroin is used for **Health products and wound healing**

136. Katia a kind of silk extracted out of **Ring & Peduncle of tasar**

137. Gicha silk is produced using **Mud pot**

138. Spun silk mills are concentrated in **West Bengal & Assam**

139. Noil yarn is **By product of spun silk**

OBJECTIVES ON SERICULTURE

1. Sericulture was practiced in China about

a) 2000 BC
b) 2500 BC
c) 3000 BC
d) None

2. The sericulture industry spread to india from

a) China
b) Japan
c) Korea
d) Tibet

3. The silkworm *Bombyx mori* has originated from

a) Bombycidae
b) Saturnidae
c) B. mandarina
d) None

4. The country which produces all 4 types of silk?

a) India
b) China
c) Japan
d) All

5. The largest producer of raw silk in the world is

a) India
b) China
c) Japan
d) All

6. Which type of Vanya silk is produced more in india

a) Tasar

b) Muga

c) Eri

d) None

7. Largest silk producing state in India is?

a) Karnataka

b) Assam

c) Andhra Pradesh

d) West Bengal

8. Largest non-mulberry silk producing state in india

a) Karnataka

b) Andhra Pradesh

c) West Bengal

d) Assam

9. All europian races are

a) Univoltine

b) Bivoltine

c) Uni and Bivoltine

d) Polyvoltine

10. All Chinese and Japanese races are

a) Univoltine

b) Bivoltine

c) Uni and Bivoltine

d) Polyvoltine

11. All tropical races are

a) Univoltine

b) Bivoltine

c) Uni and Bivoltine

d) Polyvoltine

12. The hibernating eggs are preserved in

a) Refrigerator

b) Cold storage

c) Incubator

d) None

13. The occurrence of double cocoons is common in

a) Indian race

b) Chinese race

c) Japanese race

d) None

14. The biggest cocoon market in India is at

a) Kashmir

b) Ramanagaram

c) Kolar

d) None

15. Yellow cocoon colour races of silkworm are due to

a) Presence of carotenoids and xanthophylls

b) Presence of flavonoids

c) Both a and b

d) None

16. Green cocoon colour silkworm races are due to

a) Presence of carotenoids

b) Presence of flavonoids

c) Presence of xanthophylls

d) All

17. The types of head found in silkworm is

a) Prognathous
b) Hypognathous
c) Ophisthognathous
d) None

18. Number of segments in silkworm head

a) 3
b) 6
c) 4
d) None

19. Organ of taste in silkworm is

a) Labrum
b) Maxillae
c) Hypopharynx
d) None

20. Type of Antenna found in silk moth

a) Clavate
b) Plumose
c) Geniculate
d) Pectinate

21. In silkworm 8th abdominal segment bears a median outgrowth which is called?

a) Crochets
b) Cremaster
c) Caudal horn
d) None

22. Female larvae has a pair of sex mark on the ventral side of the 8th and 9th abdominal segment is called

a) Herold gland
b) Ishiwata gland
c) Fillipis gland
d) None

23. In silk worm, the male larva has a single median opening at the junction of 8th and 9th abdominal segment is called as

a) Herold gland
b) Fillipis gland
c) Ishiwata gland
d) None

24. In silkworm digestion of which carbohydrates is not possible

a) Starch
b) Glycogen
c) Cellulose
d) None

25. The silkworm cannot synthesize

a) Amino acids
b) Fatty acids
c) Cholesterol
d) All

26. Silkworm haemolymph lacks

a) Fats
b) Calcium compound
c) Haemocyte
d) Haemoglobin

27. pH of haemolymph of silk worm is

a) 6.3-6.5

b) 7.3-8.5

c) 9.3-10.5

d) None

28. In which stage of silkworm protein level is maximum

a) Larva

b) Pupa

c) Adult

d) All

29. The respiratory system of silk worm is

a) Cutaneous

b) Tracheal

c) Both

d) None

30. On the basis of functional spiracles no of respiratory system found in silk-worm

a) Holopneustic

b) Hemipneustic

c) Peripneustic

d) None

31. The no of spiracles present in silkworm are

a) 7

b) 8

c) 9

d) None

32. The basic number of malpighian tubules in silkworm

a) Two

b) Four

c) Six

d) None

33. In silkworm the amount of uric acid excreted is about

a) 55

b) 65

c) 75

d) 85

34. Silk gland developed during which stage of silkworm development?

a) Embryonic stage

b) Larval stage

c) Pupal stage

d) None

35. Silk producing apparatus is a paired organ consisting of modified

a) Mandibular glands

b) Labial glands

c) Maxillary glands

d) None

36. Origin of silk gland is

a) Ectodermal

b) Endodermal

c) Mesodermal

d) None

37. Silkgland weight account for about

a) 30 Percent weight of the larva

b) 40 percent weight of the larva

c) 50 percent weight of the larva

d) None

38. The anterior region of the two sides of the silk glands join and open into mouth through

a) Spinning tube
b) Spinneret
c) Spinning orifice
d) None

39. The largest region of the silk gland is

a) Anterior region
b) Middle region
c) Posterior region
d) None

40. At the point where left and right anterior ends of the silk glands join there is a pair of gland called as

a) Lyonnets gland
b) Fillipis gland
c) Both A and B
d) None

41. The posterior region of the silk gland is responsible for producing the silk

a) Fibroin
b) Sericin I
c) Sericin II
d) None

42. Sericin protein is secreted from which region of the silk gland?

a) Anterior region
b) Posterior region
c) Middle region
d) None

43. Silk fibre is composed of two protein fibroin and sericin about (in percentage) respectively

a) 75, 25
b) 25,75
c) 50, 50
d) None

44. Diapause hormone in silkworm is secreted by the

a) Prothoracic gland
b) Sub oesophageal ganglion
c) Corpora cardiaca
d) None

45. Silk-worm undergo diapause during

a) Egg
b) Larval
c) Pupal
d) Adult

46. Bombyxin in silkworm are produced by

a) Juvenile hormone
b) Prothoracicotrophic hormone
c) Prothoracic gland
d) All

47. An insulin like peptide produced by silkworm is

a) Proctolin
b) Octopomine
c) Bombyxin
d) None

48. A female of silkworm lays about no of eggs

a) 200-400

b) 400-600

c) 600-800

d) None

49. The eggs of silkworm are

a) Telolecithal

b) Centrolecithal

c) Homolecithal

d) None

50. During the late stage of development of egg development, dark brown pigmentation occurs in the head and is known as

a) Head pigmentation stage

b) Eye spot stage

c) Blue egg stage

d) Both A and B

51. Pure Mysore is a popular type of which race

a) Multivoltine

b) Bivoltine

c) Univoltine

d) None

52. Hibernating eggs are preserved in

a) Cold storage

b) Oven

c) Incubator

d) Refrigerator

53. Silkworm are fond of

a) Darkness

b) Dim light

c) Strong light

d) None

54. Occurrence of double cocoon is a character of which race

a)   Multivoltine

b)   Bivoltine

c)   Univoltine

d)   None

55. Optimum humidity for Moulting is (in percentage)

a)   70-85

b)   80-85

c)   65-70

d)   75-85

56. CSR 2 is a popular (which breed)

a)   Multivoltine

b)   Bivoltine

c)   Univoltine

d)   None

57. Basic seed means

a)   Hybrid seed

b)   Commercial seed

c)   Cross breed seed

d)   Parental seed

58. Hierarchy of basic seed organization is

a)   P1, P2, P3

b)   P3, P2, P1

c)   P2, P3, P1

d)   None

59. Average numbers of egg laid by multivoltine female moth is

a)   800

b)   1000

c)   500

d)   400

60. Foundation stock is produced in

a)   P1

b)   P2

c)   P3

d)   P4

61. To achieve uniform hatching eggs are incubated at (degree Celsius)

a)   22

b)   25

c)   23

d)   27

62. Male silk worm are

a)   Homogametic

b)   Heterogametic

c)   Hemigametic

d)   None

63. Female Silk worm are

a)   Homogametic

b)   Heterogametic

c)   Hemigametic

d)   None

64. Nature of chromosomes in silk-worm

a)   Telocentric

b)   Acrocentric

c)   Metacentric

d)   None

65. Female larval genital marking in silk worm is

a)   Herold gland

b)   Ishiwata gland

c)   Alluvial gland

d)   Scent gland

66. Jaundice disease of silkworm is

a)   Pebrine

b)   Flacherie

c)   Grasserie

d)   Muscardine

67. Time required for Moulting in different instar is (in hours)

a)   5-15

b)   15-30

c)   10-20

d)   30-50

68. Temperate climate is suitable for rearing of

a)   Univoltine

b)   Bivoltine

c)   Multivoltine

d)   None

69. The average numbers of eggs in a dfl is

a)   300

b)   400

c)   500

d)   600

70. Hatching of silk-worm egg is

a)   Thermal response
b)   Photo periodic response
c)   Chemical response
d)   Mechanical response

71. The individual egg of silk worm weighs in mg

a)   1
b)   2
c)   O.6
d)   0.3

72. Optimum temperature for silkworm chawki rearing

a)   23-25
b)   26-28
c)   28-30
d)   30-32

73. Non occluded disease-causing virus is

a)   Infectious flacherie
b)   Densonucleosis
c)   Both A and B
d)   NPV

74. Occluded disease-causing virus in silk worm is

a)   Infectious flacherie
b)   Densonucleosis
c)   Both A and B
d)   NPV

75. The sperms produced by silk moth is

a) Apyrene

b) Eupyrene

c) Both

d) None

76. Inheritance of cocoon character is controlled by

a) Monogenically

b) Polygenically

c) Oligogenically

d) None

77. Optimum temperature for late age silkworm rearing is in degree Celsius

a) 23-25

b) 26-28

c) 28-30

d) 25-26

78. The Occluded RNA virus is

a) NPV

b) CPV

c) IFV

d) DNV

79. Transovarialy transmitted disease is

a) Flacherie

b) Grasserie

c) Muscardine

d) Pebrine

80. White muscardine is severe in which season

a) Summer

b) Winter

c) Rainy

d) In all seasons

81. Specific gravity of HCl for cold hydrochlorination is

a) 1.06

b) 1.10

c) 1.01

d) 1.30

82. Loose eggs are preferred in view of

a) Uniform hatching

b) High fertility

c) Easy handling

d) Quantification and high fertility

83. Commercialy reared silk-worm are

a) Tetramoulters

b) Trimoulters

c) Pentamoulters

d) None

84. Quantity of mulberry leaf ingested by silkworm larvae from brushing to ripening is

a) 50g

b) 60g

c) 80g

d) 100g

85. Largest organ in silkworm is

a) Excretory system

b) Silk gland

c) Digestive system

d) Nervous system

86. Marketing of cocoons should be done on which day of spinning

a)   3-4
b)   5-6
c)   8-9
d)   7-8

87. After oviposition acid treatment should be carried out within

a)   20hr
b)   25hr
c)   30hr
d)   40hr

88. PM x CSR2 IS popularly known as

a)   Sridevi
b)   Kaveri
c)   Nandi
d)   Kolar gold

89. Loose clumpy eggs in egg sheet is due to

a)   Pebrine
b)   NPV
c)   Flacherie
d)   Grasserie

90. Number of paired spiracles in Silk worm pupa is

a)   6
b)   7
c)   9
d)   12

91. Silkworm eggs are disinfected with

a)   Bleaching powder

b) Resham jyoti

c) Formalin

d) None

92. Labour saving silkworm rearing method is

a) Floor rearing

b) Shelf rearing

c) Shoot rearing

d) All

93. Silkworm egg production at P3 level is managed by

a) State government

b) Central government

c) LSP

d) NGOs

94. Mother moth examination was demonstrated by

a) Yokoyama

b) Tazima

c) Norton

d) Louis pasteur

95. *Bombyx mori* is

a) Holometabolous

b) Hemimetabolous

c) Heterometabolous

d) None

96. Herpes is a part of

a) Male genitalia

b) Female genitalia

c) Digestive system

d) None

97. The colour of the cocoon is imparted by pigment present in

a) Fibroin

b) Sericin

c) Both

d) None

98. Sex limited CSR breed is

a) CSR 2

b) CSR 4

c) CSR 5

d) CSR 18

99. Rangi disease of silkworm is caused by

a) Protozoa

b) Bacteria

c) Fungi

d) None

100. For pupal gut examination the part used is

a) Foregut

b) Midgut

c) Hindgut

d) None

101. Genus Morus is native of

a) Japan

b) Indo-China

c) South Koreo

d) America

102. Mulberry grows well at temperature range of (degree Celcius)

a) 13-20

b) 22-30

c) 30-35

d) 10-15

103. The Acidic Soil can be rectified by the application of

a) Gypsum

b) Lime

c) Urea

d) Nitrogen

104. The recommended doses of of NPK (kg/ha/year) for irrigated mulberry is

a) 300:120:120

b) 200:100:100

c) 100:300:100

d) 150:100:120

105. In Mulberry Sericulture the production cost towards Mulberry is (in percentage)

a) 50

b) 60

c) 25

d) 70

106. The following variety mulberry is highest yielder under irrigation

a) K2

b) M5

c) V1

d) MR2

107. Mulberry belongs to the family

a) Jack

b) Mango

c) Moringa

d) Sapota

108. Mulberry fruit is

a) Drupe

b) Sorosis

c) Hesperedium

d) Berry

109. Mulberry inflorenscence is called

a) catkin

b) spike

c) receme

d) Hypanthodium

110. Leaves are lobed in the mulberry variety

a) M5

b) Mysore local

c) S34

d) S13

111. MR1 and MR2 varieties of mulberry is suggested for management of

a) Powdery mildew

b) Rust

c) Leaf spot

d) Poor rooting

112. Ideoblasts in mulberry leaf contain

a) Calcium carbonate

b) Urea

c) Magnesium nitrate

d) Potassium Carbonate

113. Highest chromosomal number is seen in

a) *Morus alba*

b) *Morus nigra*

c) *Morus rubra*

d) *Morus indica*

114. Tachinid flies are the

a) Pathogens

b) Parasitoids

c) Predators

d) All of these

115. Serious endo-larval parasitoid of the silkworm

a) Uzifly

b) Dermestid beetle

c) *Nesolynx thymus*

d) None

116. The life cycle of Uzifly is completed in (days)

a) 18-22

b) 25-30

c) 40-50

d) None

117. The biological control of Uzifly is

a) *Nesolynx thymus*

b) *Attagenus faciatus*

c) *Anthrenus flavips*

d) None

118. The number of eggs laid by uzifly per host larva is

a) 2-3

b) 4-6

c) 8-10

d) None

119. Recommended dose of ectopupal parasitoid *N. thymus* for management of uzifly

a) @50000 adults/100dfls

b) @1 lakh adults/100 dfls

c) @2 lakh adults/100 dfls

d) None

120. Japanese uzifly lays eggs on

a) Silkworm body

b) Mulberry Leaf

c) Silk moth

d) All

121. *Dermestes ater* is reported to attack

a) Dried fishes

b) Leather goods

c) Silk

d) All

122. *Dermestes ater* is not posing any problem to

a) Green cocoons

b) Dried Cocoons

c) Raw silk

d) All

123. Which Enzyme is used as a marker in silkworm breeding programme

a) Lipase

b) Trehalase

c) Amylase

d) None

124. Preservation of qualities of parental races is the fundamental principle

a) Line breeding
b) Cross breeding
c) Mutation breeding
d) None

125. The diploid chromosome number of silk worm *Bombyx mori*

a) 54
b) 56
c) 58
d) 60

126. The chromosome number of Tasar silkworm *Antheraeae mylitta* is

a) 62
b) 60
c) 58
d) 56

127. The Chromosome number of Muga silkworm is

a) 60
b) 30
c) 28
d) 20

128. The chromosome number of Eri silk worm is

a) 60
b) 30
c) 28
d) 20

129. The loss of vigour is a consequence of

a) Inbreeding

b) Outbreeding

c) Heterosis

d) None

130. The cross of the F1 with the recessive homozygous parent is referred as

a) Test cross

b) Top cross

c) Three way cross

d) None

131. Best period for bottom prunning of mulberry in south india is

a) july aug

b) nov-dec

c) feb-march

d) may-june

132. The type of sex chromosome in male and female silkworm is

a) ZZ, ZW

b) WW, ZZ

c) ZW, ZZ

d) None

133. Sex limited race of silkworm

a) CS3

b) CSR 8

c) CSR 18

d) All

134. The development of an individual from the female gamete without fertilization is known as

a) Fertilization

b) Parthenocarpy

c) Parthenogenesis

d) None

135. Parthenogenesis in silkworm is induced by

a) Hot water treatment

b) HCL treatment

c) Both

d) None

136. Improvement in the performance of selected lines over normal original population is known as

a) Genetic advance

b) Genetic equillibrium

c) Genetic erosion

d) None

137. Gradual dissapearance of various forms of a cultivated species and of its wild relatives is called

a) Genetic advance

b) Genetic equillibrium

c) Genetic erosion

d) None

138. Mulberry variety recommended for Chawki silkworm rearing

a) M5

b) RFS 175

c) DD

d) S 36

139. The recommended FYM for rainfed mulberry is (tonnes/ha/year)

a) 10

b) 5

c) 15

d) 20

140. Which of the following is required for hybridization in mulberry plants

a) Male sterile plants

b) Self-incompatibility

c) Emasculation

d) None

141. The most suitable soil type of mulberry is

a) Sandy loam

b) Medium black

c) Laterite

d) Red loam

142. Mulberry is pollinated largely by

a) insects

b) wind

c) self-pollination

d) birds

143. leaf yield of V1 per hacter per annum under irrigated condition (kg)

a) 35

b) 60

c) 25

d) 15

144. The ideal pH for mulberry cultivation is

a) 7.5-8.5

b) 6.6-7.5

c) 8.5-10

d) >10

145. Species of mulberry distributed in india

a) *M. cathyana*
b) *M. nigra*
c) *M. indica*
d) none

146. Laceration of mulberry leaf epidermal cells resulting in shrivelling is due to

a) Mites
b) Thrips
c) Jassids
d) Whitefly

147. Fertigation efficiency is more in

a) Drip irrigation
b) Furrow irrigation
c) Flood irrigation
d) Sprinkler irrigation

148. M5 was evolved from

a) MR1
b) MR2
c) K2
d) Mysore local

149. Mulberry belongs to the genus

a) Morus
b) Artocarpus
c) Syzizium
d) Plumeria

150. Virgin and sandy soils attract the infestation of

a) Termites

b) Grasshopper

c) Nematodes

d) Cutworms

151. Who is the largest producer of Tasar Silk

a) India

b) China

c) Japan

d) All of these

152. The domesticated non mulberry silkworm is

a) Eri

b) Tasar

c) Muga

d) All of these

153. Traditional Tasar silk is produced by

a) *A. proylei*

b) *A. mylitta*

c) *A. pernyi*

d) All

154. Which tasar strain is reared in jammu kashmir?

a) *A. proylei*

b) *A. mylitta*

c) *A. pernyi*

d) None

155. The silk obtained from *Attacus atlas* is known known as

a) Dupion silk

b) fagara silk

c) Spun silk

d) None

156. The reelability of tasar cocoon is

a) 25%
b) 50%
c) 75%
d) None

157. Open mouthed cocoons are spun by

a) Tasar
b) Eri
c) Muga
d) None

158. Yield loss of tasar crop through diseases is

a) 20%
b) 30%
c) 40%
d) None

159. Which is the common disease that affects tasar worms

a) Microsporodiosis
b) Bacteriosis
c) Polyhydrosis
d) All

160. The average filament length of tasar cocoon is

a) 500m
b) 800m
c) 1500m
d) None

161. Which of the following non mulberry silkworms are reared indoor

a) Tasar

b) Eri

c) Muga

d) None

162. Which of the following cocoons are used in hand spinning for making spun silk?

a) Tasar

b) Eri

c) Muga

d) None

163. What is the natural colour of tasar cocoons

a) Yellow

b) Grey

c) White

d) All

164. Coan silk is produced by

a) *Pachypasa otus*

b) *Attacus atlas*

c) *Philosamia ricini*

d) None

165. Anaphe silk is produced by

a) *Anaphe panda*

b) *Pachypasa otus*

c) *Philosamia ricini*

d) None

166. Which of the following silk is not used in textile industry?

a) Mussel silk

b) Fagara silk

c) Spider silk

d) None

167. Peduncle formation is laid down by connecting the ring to the top of hammock strands of silk by

a) Tasar silkworm

b) Eri silkworm

c) Muga silk worm

d) None

168. The type of diapause occurs in tasar silkworm is

a) egg diapause

b) pupal diapause

c) adult diapause

d) both A and B

169. Egg diapause occurs in

a) *Bombyx mori*

b) *A. yamamai*

c) *A. mylitta*

d) Both A and B

170. The yarn prepared by handout of tasar cocoons is called

a) Gicha

b) Grege

c) Georgette

d) None

171. The muga silkworm is

a) Univoltine

b) Bivoltine

c) Multivoltine

d) None

172. Halflong green is a

a) Tasar silkworm
b) Muga silkworm
c) Eri silkworm
d) None

173. Averege quantity of spun silk yarn by single eri cocoon?

a) 0.3g
b) 0.5g
c) 1.5g
d) none

174. Mussel silk is produced by

a) *Attacus atlas*
b) *Pachypasa otus*
c) *Pinna squamosa*
d) None

175. The silk produced *Nephila medagascarensis* is known

a) Mussel silk
b) Coan silk
c) Anaphe silk
d) Spider silk

176. What is the haploid chromosome number of *Antheraea mylitta*

a) 14
b) 30
c) 31
d) none

177. The supression of homologous gene is known as

a) Gene targeting

b) Gene Silencing

c) Transposon tagging

d) None

178. Both DNA and RNA have a

a) Negative charge

b) Positive charge

c) Neutral charge

d) None

179. Transgenic mulberry plants were generated by expression of

a) Beta A gene

b) Fad7 gene

c) Hva1 gene

d) None

180. The first world transgenic mulberry plant with drought and salinity tolerance was developed by

a) Delhi university

b) National institute of agrobiological sciences

c) Biotechnology research centre CAAS Beijing

d) None

181. The first transgenic silkwork was developed in 2000 using

a) Luciferase gene

b) Insulin

c) Green fluorescent protein gene

d) Spider silk protein gene

182. Transgenic silkworm expressing spider dragline silk protein was established in

a) 2000

b) 2005

c) 2014

d) 2016

183. In India, the first transgenic silkworms resistant to BmNPV virus was developed by

a) Indian institute of sciences, Bangalore
b) Central Sericulture research institute
c) CDFD Hyderabad
d) CSRTI, Berhampore

184. Transgenic silkworms have been recently generated to integrate the foreign genes of interest into the chromosomes of germline cells using

a) A Piggy Bac transposon vector
b) Bac to Bac Expression system
c) *E. coli*
d) None

185. Which of the following is a dominant marker

a) RAPD
b) AFLP
c) SSR
d) None

186. Microsatellites are also known as

a) RAPDs
b) AFLPs
c) SSR
d) VNTRs

187. Minisatellites are also known as

a) RAPDs
b) AFLPs
c) SSR

d) VNTRs

188. The type of mulberry variety evolved through chemical mutagenesis in India

a) S36
b) S41
c) S54
d) All

189. In Japan which variety of mulberry is evolved through chemical mutagenesis

a) KNG
b) Ichinose
c) Kokuso
d) All

190. Which of the mulberry variety is a polyploidy

a) *M. nigra*
b) *M. cathyana*
c) *M. serrata*
d) All

191. Which of the following ploidy in mulberry is superior in leaf yield and quality

a) Diploids
b) triploids
c) Tetraploids
d) All

192. *Morus nigra* has docosaploidy with chromosome number (2n=???)

a) 28
b) 308
c) 256
d) 56

193. The chromosome number of diploid mulberry variety is (2n=?????)

a) 28

b) 308

c) 256

d) 56

194. Which country holds largest mulberry germplasm collection in the world?

a) India

b) China

c) Japan

d) none

195. In India mulberry inflorescence length is higher in

a) *M. alba*

b) *M. indica*

c) *M. serrata*

d) None

196. The complete nucleotide sequence of mulberry chloroplast genome is

a) 158484 bp

b) 25678 bp

c) 87339 bp

d) none

197. Which of the cultivar are developed through open pollinated hybrid selection

a) K 2

b) MR 2

c) S 13

d) All

198. *Trichogramma chilonis* is a biocontrol agent of

a) Mealy bug

b) Leaf roller

c)   Thrips

d)   All

199. Tukra disease is caused by

a)   *Diapharina pulverulentalis*

b)   *Euproctis irrorata*

c)   *Maconellicoccus hirsutus*

d)   None

200. Violet root rot of mulberry is caused by

a)   *Helicobasidium mompa*

b)   *Rosellina necatrix*

c)   *Polyporus hispidus*

d)   None

201. When can an entire branch containing leaves to be fed to the larva of silk worm?

a) Neonate

b) 2nd Instar

c) 3rd instar

d) 4th and 5th instar

202. The queen of textile is?

a) Cotton

b) Silk

c) Wool

d) Linen

203. Central Muga Eri Research and training institute is in?

a) Manipur

b) Assam

c) West Bengal

d) Odisha

204. Which of the following is known as tassar silkworm?

a) Antheraea proylei

b) Antheraea assamensis

c) Samia ricini

d) Antheraea mylitta

205. Mulberry is pollinated by?

a) Insect

b) Wind

c) Rain

d) Irrigation water

206. Hibernating eggs are stored in?

a) Cold storage

b) Freeze

c) BOD

d) None

207. Mulberry grows properly in the temperature range of (in degree celsius)?

a) 15-20

b) 20-30

c) 30-35

d) 35-40

208. The high yielding variety of mulberry strain is?

a) M5

b) S54

c) S13

d) V1

209. The optimum pH suitable for mulberry cultivation?

a) 5.2-5.8

b) 6.2-6.8

c) 6.7-7.8

d) 4.5-5.9

210. Soil suitable for mulberry cultivation?

a) Red loamy

b) Alluvial

c) Saline

d) Black cotton

211. Highest ripening day of mature worms in muga rearing is?

a) Bhorpak

b) Jhali

c) Kharika

d) Chaloni

212. The most common method of propagation in mulberry is?

a) Seeds

b) Stem cutting

c) Grafting

d) Layering

213. Mulberry plant is?

a) Annual

b) Biennial

c) Perrenial

d) Decennial

214. Mulberry belongs to family?

a) Malvaceae

b) Compositae

c) Moraceae

d) Leguminaceae

215. Major weed in Mulberry Garden is?

a) Parthenium

b) Datura

c) Achyranthus

d) Euphorbia

216. Inflorescence of mulberry is?

a) Head

b) Catkin

c) Umbel

d) Verticillaster

217. Mulberry grows well in a rainfall of?

a) 500-1000mm

b) 100-700mm

c) 200-500mm

d) 600-2500mm

218. Mulberry leaf is exclusively used for rearing of silkworm larvae due to presence of?

a) Carbohydrates

b) Morin

c) Lipids

d) Vit-A

219. Tukra disease is caused by?

a) Grass hopper

b) Mealy bug

c) Nematode

d) Cutworm

220. The silk is first discovered in country?

a) India

b) China

c) Japan

d) America

221. The silkworm respiration is carried out by ?

a) Lungs

b) Gills

c) Skin

d) Spiracle

222. Number of pairs of malpighian tubules present in silkworm?

a) 3

b) 6

c) 4

d) 5

223. Numbers of pairs of ovaries and ovarioles present in silkworm?

a) 1 and 4

d) 4 and 1

c) 2 and 4

d) 4 and 2

224. The female silkworm larvae can be identified by?

a) Ishiwata gland

b) Fillipis gland

c) Lynnots gland

d) Scent glands

225. Number of pairs of spiracles present in larvae, pupa and adults in silkworm respectively?

a) 9,7,6

b) 6,7,8

c) 8,7,6

d) None

226. Tassar diapause occurs during?

a) Egg

b) Pupa

c) Both

d) None

227. The number of instars in silkworm larva?

a) 3

b) 2

c) 5

d) 4

228. The caudal horn is present in which segment?

a) 3

b) 9

c) 5

d) 4

229. Fibroin is secreted from which part of silk gland?

a) Anterior

b) Posterior

c) Middle

d) All

230. Non mulberry silkworms belongs to family?

a) Saturnidae

b) Bombycidae

c) Coccinelidae

d) Coccidae

231. Chromosome number (2n) of mulberry silkworm?

a) 56

b) 28

c) 14

d) 64

232. Chromosome number (2n) of mulberry plant is?

a) 28

b) 56

c) 30

d) 64

233. Shortest molting period of silkworm is?

a) 1st moult

b) 2nd moult

c) 3rd moult

d) 4th moult

234. Pupal gut examination is done to detect?

a) Grasserie

b) Pebrine

c) Flacherie

d) Sotto

235. Artificial hatching of silkworm is done by using?

a) H2SO4

b) HCl

c) HCOOH

d) CH3COOH

236. The sex chromosome of silkworm are?

a) ZW

b) XY

c) XX

d) WW

237. The larval life of silkworm?

a) 20-24 days

b) 24-28 days

c) 30-35 days

d) 35-40 days

238. The cocoon that yield Spun silk is?

a) Eri

b) Tasar

c) Muga

d) Mulberry

39. Silk reeled from double cocoon is?

a) Dupion silk

b) Banaras silk

c) Mysore silk

d) Kora silk

240. One box of loose eggs contain?

a) 10,000

b) 5000

c) 20,000

d) 30,000

241. The weight increase from first to fifth instar larva is?

a) 5000 times

b) 6000 times

c) 7000 times

d) 10000 times

242. Common type of mountage in South india?

a) Chandrika

b) Bottle brush

c) Straw

d) Rotary

243. Fillipis gland is associated with?

a) Silk gland

b) Scent gland

c) Prothoracic gland

d) Corpora allata

244. Scientist discovered Mother moth examination?

a) Toyoma

b) Mendel

c) Tazima

d) Louis pasteur

245. The stage of egg just before hatching is called as?

a) Blue head stage

b) Red head stage

c) yellow head stage

d) Green head stage

246. The surface disinfection of egg sheet is done by?

a) Formalin

b) RKO

c) Lime

d) Bleaching powder

247. Hanging disease is caused by?

a) Virus

b) Fungus

c) Bacteria

d) protozoa

248. Moth emerges from cocoon on which day?

a) 10th

b) 7th

c) 5th

d) 8th

249. The innermost layer of cocoon is known as?

a) Floss

b) Palade

c) Fibroin

d) Sericin

250. The outermost layer of cocoon is known as?

a) Floss

b) Palade

c) Fibroin

d) Sericin

ANSWER KEY FOR SERICULTURE

1	2	3	4	5	6	7	8	9	10	11	12	13	14	15
B	D	C	A	B	C	A	D	A	C	D	B	C	B	A

16	17	18	19	20	21	22	23	24	25	26	27	28	29	30
B	B	B	B	D	C	B	A	C	C	D	A	A	B	C

31	32	33	34	35	36	37	38	39	40	41	42	43	44	45
C	C	D	A	B	A	B	B	C	C	A	C	A	B	A

46	47	48	49	50	51	52	53	54	55	56	57	58	59	60
B	C	B	B	D	A	A	B	B	C	B	D	B	D	B

61	62	63	64	65	66	67	68	69	70	71	72	73	74	75
B	A	B	C	A	C	B	A	B	B	C	B	C	D	C

76	77	78	79	80	81	82	83	84	85	86	87	88	89	90
B	A	B	D	B	B	D	A	A	B	B	A	D	A	B

91	92	93	94	95	96	97	98	99	100	101	102	103	104	105
C	C	A	D	A	A	B	D	B	B	B	B	B	A	B

106	107	108	109	110	111	112	113	114	115	116	117	118	119	120
C	A	B	A	B	A	A	B	B	A	A	A	A	B	B

121	122	123	124	125	126	127	128	129	130	131	132	133	134	135
D	A	B	A	B	A	B	C	A	A	A	A	D	C	C

136	137	138	139	140	141	142	143	144	145	146	147	148	149	150
A	C	D	A	C	D	B	B	B	C	B	A	D	A	A

151	152	153	154	155	156	157	158	159	160	161	162	163	164	165
B	A	B	A	B	B	B	C	D	B	B	B	D	A	A

166	167	168	169	170	171	172	173	174	175	176	177	178	179	180
C	A	D	D	A	C	B	B	C	D	C	B	A	C	A

181	182	183	184	185	186	187	188	189	190	191	192	193	194	195
C	C	C	A	A	C	D	D	D	D	B	B	A	B	C

196	197	198	199	200	201	202	203	204	205	206	207	208	209	210
A	D	B	C	B	C	B	B	D	B	A	B	D	B	A

211	212	213	214	215	216	217	218	219	220	221	222	223	224	225

A	B	C	C	A	B	D	B	B	B	D	A	A	A	A
226	**227**	**228**	**229**	**230**	**231**	**232**	**233**	**234**	**235**	**236**	**237**	**238**	**239**	**240**
C	C	B	B	A	A	A	B	B	B	A	B	A	A	C

241	**242**	**243**	**244**	**245**	**246**	**247**	**248**	**249**	**250**
D	A	A	D	A	A	A	A	B	A

About Authors

Aarthi Nekkanti completed her master's degree in Entomology from ICAR-Indian Agricultural Research Institute, New Delhi, where she focused on investigating the molecular mechanisms of virus-vector interactions, specifically between the chili leaf curl virus and *Bemisia tabaci*. She has published her research findings in various esteemed national and international journals and has received multiple awards for presenting her work at various conferences. Throughout her academic career, she was also awarded various scholarships. Currently, she is pursuing Ph.D. in Entomology at Indira Gandhi Krishi Vishwavidyalaya, Raipur, Chhattisgarh, where her research centers on exploring the biocontrol potential of *Bacillus thuringiensis* in insect pest management. All of her Ph.D. research work is being conducted at ICAR- National Bureau of Agricultural Insect Resources, Bengaluru, Karnataka.

Ms. J. Komal, presently working as Scientist in Central Silk Board. She had graduated with distinction from Agricultural college, Aswaraopeta (PJTSAU) in 2019. She has got University Silver Medal for highest O.G.P.A in Plant Protection. She had secured all India 3rd rank in Entomology and awarded with JRF by ICAR and completed her Master's in Entomology from ICAR-Indian Agricultural Research Institute. She has secured prestigious IARI gold medal. She has bagged best M. Sc thesis award at a national conference organized by the well renowned Society of Plant Protection Sciences (SPPS). Later, secured all India 8th rank in SRF Crop sciences exam by ICAR. She also qualified ICAR-NET. She has also been an author in many international and national publications.